DEFICIT HYSTERIA

DEFICIT HYSTERIA

A Common Sense Look at America's Rush to Balance the Budget

Arthur Benavie

Westport, Connecticut
London

Library of Congress Cataloging-in-Publication Data

Benavie, Arthur.
    Deficit hysteria : a common sense look at America's rush to
balance the budget / Arthur Benavie.
      p. cm.
    Includes bibliographical references and index.
    ISBN 0–275–96308–X (alk. paper)
    1. Budget—United States.   2. Budget deficits—United States.
3. Government spending policy—United States.   I. Title.
HJ2051.B46   1998
339.5'23'0973—dc21   98–14926

British Library Cataloguing in Publication Data is available.

Library of Congress Catalog Card Number: 98–14926
ISBN: 0–275–96308–X

First published in 1998

Praeger Publishers, 88 Post Road West, Westport, CT 06881
An imprint of Greenwood Publishing Group, Inc.

Printed in the United States of America

♾™

The paper used in this book complies with the
Permanent Paper Standard issued by the National
Information Standards Organization (Z39.48–1984).

10 9 8 7 6 5 4 3 2 1

Copyright Acknowledgments

The author and publisher are grateful for permission to reproduce portions of the
following copyrighted material:

James D. Savage, *Balanced Budgets and American Politics* (Ithaca, N.Y.: Cornell
University Press, 1988). Copyright © 1988 by Cornell University. Used by permission
of the publisher, Cornell University Press.

James M. Rock, ed., *Debt and the Twin Deficits Debate* (Mountain View, Calif.:
Bristlecone Books, Mayfield, 1991). Permission granted by James M. Rock, copyright
holder.

To my wife Marcy,
with all my love.

Contents

Acknowledgments

I owe a debt of gratitude to Stanley Black and Richard Froyen, my colleagues in the Economics Department at the University of North Carolina, who have not only borne my rantings and ravings on this topic over the years but also critiqued an earlier version of the manuscript. (When I told Stan Black that I felt guilty suspending my research to write a book explaining the deficit to the general public, he cheered me up by reminding me that that effort was simply a different kind of teaching.)

Other economists have encouraged me with their advice and support and have cared enough to take the trouble to read and comment on sections of the manuscript that I sent unsolicited: my appreciation and thanks to Robert Eisner, John Kenneth Galbraith, Robert Heilbroner, Franco Modigliani, and Robert Solow. My thanks also to Edwin Yoder for his counsel and encouragement. Finally, I'm grateful to my friends Sid Simon, Ed Baxter, Bill Keech, and George Richards, who not only pushed me to write this book but read much of it, supplying abundant enthusiasm as well as criticism.

Without question, though, my greatest debt of gratitude is to my wife, Marcy Lansman, a gifted writer who spent months working with me on this book. To the extent that the style is lucid and compelling, she deserves much of the credit.

DEFICIT HYSTERIA

Introduction

June, 1998: For now, we're safe. We have eluded that horrifying monster called "the deficit." But one false move and we could fall back into its grip again, or so the politicians and pundits would have us believe. Black holes, time bombs, arterial bleeding; these are only a few of the nightmarish images that have been used to describe the deficit. Herblock has drawn it as a Frankenstein monster with "MADE IN USA" tattooed on his forehead.

During the 1980s and early 1990s, as the deficit soared, many were convinced that economic disaster lay just around the corner. And still today, with surpluses on the horizon, our country is enslaved by a powerful myth: that the deficit is a sinister force, rotting the material and moral foundations of our society, a blight that must be wiped out as soon as possible no matter what the cost. Politicians are falling all over themselves to assure us they won't let it happen again.

The truth is that *the size of the deficit (or surplus) alone tells us nothing about the health of our economy. Only when we consider how the government is using its revenues—whether they are derived from taxes or borrowing—can we evaluate our economic policy.* Fear of the deficit, on the other hand, can cause real harm, by tying our government's hands and blinding us to the *true* indicators of our country's economic well-being: employment, inflation, productivity, and the gap between the rich and poor. Only if we overcome our deficit phobia will we be able to formulate policy conducive to our economic well-being.

As I send this book to the press the deficit appears to be vanishing and budget surpluses are currently projected for the next several years, to be followed, however, by huge deficits again when the baby boomers begin to retire around 2010. *A deficit is simply a negative surplus, so the ideas developed here apply to both; that is, increasing the deficit has the same impact on the economy as reducing the surplus.* No matter what the projections are—and they change constantly—we need a rational understanding of how the deficit and the surplus are related to our economic health. The goal of this book is to promote this understanding.

1. WHAT IS THE DEFICIT?

Many people have only the fuzziest of idea what the deficit is and how it is related to the public debt.

Whenever the government spends more than it collects in taxes, it must borrow the difference. *The deficit is the amount borrowed.* The government borrows by selling securities (e.g., Treasury bills) to the public.[1] In buying these securities, the public is lending money to the government.

The stock of government securities held by the public is called the public (or national) debt. Every year that the government runs a deficit, the public debt increases by the amount of the deficit.

Conversely, every year the government runs a surplus—that is, spends less than it collects in taxes—the public debt decreases by the amount of the surplus. A surplus means the government is channeling its excess taxes to the private sector by retiring the public debt.

2. HOW BIG IS THE PUBLIC DEBT?

Do you have a debt? A mortgage, say, or a car loan? Is your debt "big"? That depends on your ability to meet the payments. If you're carrying a $100,000 mortgage on an income of $75,000 a year, your debt may not seem very large. But if your income were to drop from $100,000 to $25,000, the same mortgage might become a strain.

A similar logic applies to the public debt. Just as your debt is backed by your income, the public debt is backed by the nation's income. The usual measure of the *burden of the debt* is the ratio of the debt to national income. The most common measure of national income is the gross domestic product (GDP), which is the total value of output (and income) produced in the United States.[2] In 1995 the GDP was about $7.2 trillion, and the public debt was about $3.6 trillion.[3] Thus, the ratio of the public debt to GDP was about 50%.

Many people believe the debt burden is heavier today than it has ever been. Not true. In fact, the debt–GDP ratio has been higher—much higher, as you can see in Figure 1. In 1953, for example, the debt–GDP ratio was 60%. In 1946, the public debt actually exceeded the nation's income!

Suppose we ran permanent deficits. Wouldn't the burden of the debt grow? Not necessarily. What if we incurred continuously *increasing* deficits every year? Wouldn't that cause the debt burden to increase? Again, not necessarily! The reason? Our GDP is also projected to grow. Given a broadly accepted assumption about GDP growth in the United States, our 1995 deficit of $164 billion could grow by, say, 5% a year, and it can be shown that our debt–GDP ratio would decline to 46%.[4]

Politicians and pundits warn us constantly that the public debt will impoverish our children and grandchildren.[5] History shows that this dire prediction need not come true. Even with a debt–GDP ratio of 114% in 1946, our standard of living moved up at a remarkably brisk pace over the next 25 years!

3. WHO HOLDS THE PUBLIC DEBT?

For every debtor there has to be a creditor. The creditors of the U.S. government as of March 31, 1995, are shown in Table 1. These are the institutions and individuals who have lent our government money and are consequently holding claims against the government. These claims consist of various types of interest-yielding government securities. They are assets to the holders. In fact, they are the most highly prized of assets, since they are backed by the reputation of the U.S. government and hence bear a negligible risk of default.

What exactly are these securities? They are IOUs of the government that promise to pay the holder a fixed amount of money at a maturity date along with fixed payments at specified times, called coupon or interest payments. Most of them are marketable; that is, they can be bought and sold at any time at their market price. The rest are nonmarketable, like savings bonds. The marketable securities on March 31, 1995, were made up of Treasury bills (24%), notes (60%), and bonds (16%). A Treasury bill has a short maturity, usually 30 to 90 days. A note has a maturity of a year. Bonds have the longest maturity, up to as long as 30 years. One characteristic of these marketable securities is that their prices

Figure 1
The Burden of the Public Debt

Public Debt as a Percentage of GDP

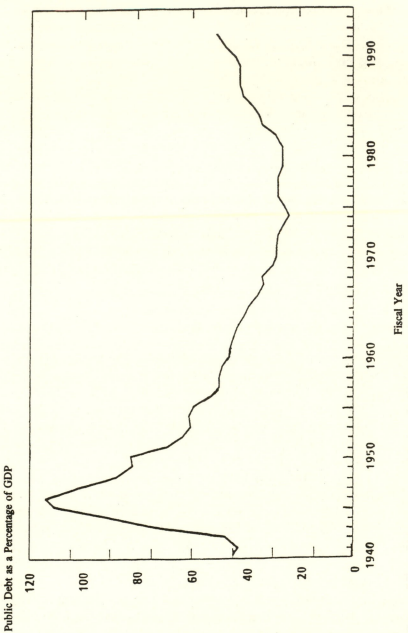

Fiscal Year

Source: Office of Management and Budget for 1940–1992.

Table 1
Gross National Debt of the U.S. Treasury by Holder, March 31, 1995

	$Billions	% of Total
U.S. Government Agencies and Trust Funds*	1,624.0	33.4
Financial Institutions**	1,688.2	34.7
State and Local Treasuries	480.0	9.9
Individuals	342.8	7.0
Foreign and International	728.1	15.0
Total Gross Debt*	**4,864.1**	

*Includes $369.3 billion held by the Federal Reserve Banks.
**Includes commercial banks, insurance companies, money market funds, savings and
    loan associations, nonprofit institutions, credit unions, mutual savings banks, cor-
    porate pension trust funds, and dealers and brokers.
***Components do not sum precisely to total due to rounding error.

Source: Federal Reserve Bulletin, September 1995, table A30.

move inversely with interest rates; that is, if interest rates rise, the market
prices of these securities fall, and vice versa.

Notice that a third of the gross national debt, over $1.6 trillion, is held
by the government itself. One branch of the government has borrowed
from another. No future tax burden to the public is involved. Interest
and principal payments on this portion of the debt are simply intragov-
ernmental transfers, of concern only to the accountants.

The gross debt exaggerates the national debt that should be of concern
to the public. Yet, you will frequently see the gross debt falsely proclaimed as the debt that our children will inherit. The national debt
clocks, for example, invariably display the gross debt. As the *Economist*
reported on June 3, 1995:

For the past six years the national debt clock, a vast electronic scoreboard in
mid-town Manhattan, has been clocking up the size of America's overdraft,
second by $10,000 second, day by $860m day. By the time Seymour Durst, the
clock's creator and a New York property developer, died a few weeks ago at
the age of 81, the tally had hit almost $4.9 trillion. . . .

When, in 1992, Paul Tsongas and Warren Rudman launched the Concord
Coalition, a body devoted to balancing the budget by 2002, they held the press
conference in the shadow of Mr. Durst's debt clock. Since then, the coalition
has built its own mobile clock. . . .

Clock-watching has caught on in the Capitol, too. John Kasich, the slash-and-burn Republican chairman of the House Budget Committee, has recently presided over committee meetings with a digital debt clock . . . whirring away behind him.

The relevant debt is the public debt, that is, the debt held outside the government. The public debt on March 31, 1995, was the gross debt of about $4.9 trillion minus the government-held debt of $1.6 trillion, which was about $3.2 trillion.

Table 1 also shows that individual citizens hold only 7% of the debt, whereas 34.7% is held by financial institutions such as banks or insurance companies, and 9.9% is held by state and local governments. The services provided by these financial institutions and governments are financed in part by the interest they earn on their U.S. government securities.

Note also that 15% of the gross debt was held by foreigners. It is interesting that this percentage has changed little since 1980 in spite of the huge deficits incurred after that. Foreigners held 13.9% of our debt in 1980.

Looking at the owners of government securities can help us appreciate the crucial functions performed by our national debt.[6] Where could individuals, corporations, insurance companies, and pension funds find an alternative investment of such safety and high quality for their excess revenues? What other securities would be politically suitable for purchase and sale by our Federal Reserve in its adjustment of interest rates? Finally, note that while our children will inherit the public debt, they will also be the holders of most of these securities as a part of their wealth.[7]

4. SHOULD WE BE ALARMED?

Suppose a friend wanted to borrow $10,000 and asked if you thought that was a good idea. To advise your friend, you would need to know how the money was to be spent. You might react differently if the loan was going for college tuition than if it was going for a vacation in Bermuda. Similar reasoning holds for the government. The impact of government borrowing depends on how the funds are to be spent—whether to upgrade labor skills, improve our transportation system, raise bureaucrats' salaries, increase farm price supports, buy nuclear submarines, or any of a thousand other purposes. Yet people often condemn deficit spending without considering what the borrowed money is going for.

The existence of deficits, even growing deficits, is not, in and of itself, a reason for alarm. Lending to the government could be the best use for those funds.

5. WHY DEFICIT PANIC?

Back in the days of huge deficits, people were constantly approaching me with questions. How soon before our country goes bankrupt? Is it true that a huge part of our grandchildren's income will go toward interest on the debt? When I failed to endorse their catastrophic scenarios, they were incredulous, even shocked. Then why are people so alarmed? they wanted to know. And why weren't economists doing anything to put their fears to rest?

One reason for deficit hysteria was the common belief that deficits can cause our government to become insolvent. People draw a false analogy between individual debt and government debt. True, if *you* borrow too much, you're in trouble; you may be forced into bankruptcy. Not so for the U.S. government. Since the government has the power to tax and an unlimited credit line, it can always meet its debts. The notion that borrowing can bankrupt our government is false.[8]

Another reason people were alarmed is that the deficit rose so steeply during the 1980s and early 1990s, and that much of the money borrowed appeared to be used for the benefit of present, rather than future, generations.[9] Many shared the judgment of Harvard economist Benjamin Friedman that "America has thrown itself a party and billed the tab to the future."[10] Had the borrowed money been used for education, environmental cleanup, and children's health rather than for defense, Social Security, and Medicare, people might have viewed deficits more favorably.

An additional factor, I believe, is that many, including some economists, have played on people's ignorance and fear of deficits to push their own political views. I once asked an economist friend why he was telling people deficits were dangerous when he knew that was not necessarily the case. His answer went something like this: "What I would really like to tell them is that I think the government is too big, and I want more resources left to the private sector. But, if I put it *that* way, no one will listen. When I tell people that deficits will bankrupt their children, they pay attention.'' (My friend knows that big government and big deficits are very different things.)

Deficit hysteria has become so widespread that few public figures are brave enough to resist it. Politicians run the risk of being driven out of office if they fail to condemn the deficit. Economists who know better often fall into line. One well-known, Washington-based economist told me he was afraid people would think he was crazy if he tried to explain that deficits could be good or bad. Instead he kept quiet.

Many (but not all) pundits feed the frenzy. Listen to *Newsweek* columnist Robert Samuelson (not to be confused with the Nobel Prize-winning economist Paul Samuelson): "Why bother with deficits then? The answer is that there are distant dangers, even if we don't know precisely what they are or when they might occur.''[11] Scary, eh?

Finally, many who condemn the deficit are referred to as economists but have actually had little training in the subject. After all, anyone can call him or herself an economist. In addition, economics has a lot of different specialties, many having little to do with deficits. So, simply because someone is an economist doesn't mean that person understands the economics of the deficit.

By now you may be wondering whether I'm the only economist who's talking this way about the deficit. Not by a long shot. In fact, I'm in good company. Listen to what some well-known economists have said:

By themselves, debts and deficits are neither good nor bad. They are *means* to an end, which may or may not be constructive. (Peter Peterson[12])

Governments may borrow rather than tax because it is economically sensible and rational to do so, exactly as is the case with households or corporations. (Robert Heilbroner and Peter Bernstein[13])

The federal debt is not a measure of economic suffering or even, in any clear way, related to it. (Robert Eisner[14])

There remain those government expenditures which are intended to improve future well-being and economic growth or which so serve. Here, borrowing is not only legitimate but socially and economically desirable. (John Kenneth Galbraith[15])

The views I put forward in this book are not extreme. They reflect mainstream economic thinking.

6. AREN'T DEFICITS HARMFUL?

What about some of the other claims politicians and pundits have been making? Won't deficits raise interest rates? Cause inflation? Create a trade deficit? Crowd out private investment? Impoverish your children?

The answer to all of these questions is either no or not necessarily.

Consider a common misconception: "Deficits increase the tax burden on your children." It is true, of course, that running a deficit will increase the public debt and thereby increase interest payments on that debt. To raise the funds for these interest payments, your taxes and those of your children will be increased.

But what have I really told you if I say your taxes will increase? Nothing! With no other information, the amount of your future taxes is a meaningless number. You must also know something about your ability to pay those taxes. The point is this: *While a deficit implies additional future taxes, it can also boost future income. If the borrowed funds are spent productively, your income and that of your children may be raised by more than enough to cover the interest payments. Running a deficit in the present may cause your future standard of living to go up instead of down.*

How can deficits increase the nation's future income? The borrowed money could be used to increase the productivity of the labor force, that is, increase the goods and services the average worker can produce in an hour's work. If the government spends its borrowed funds on such projects as training workers or developing new technologies, productivity may be enhanced, and the nation's future ability to generate output will be increased.

On the downside, deficits could also decrease our future income. If the government borrows for spending that generates only current benefits (such as salaries or Social Security), then businesses will be deprived of funds that could be used for investments (such as equipment or research and development) that would increase worker productivity. In this case, our children will be saddled with additional taxes and a decreased ability to pay those taxes.[16]

A deficit can be either a blessing or a curse, depending on how the government spends the borrowed money.

7. THE DANGERS OF DEFICIT PANIC

While deficits are not necessarily harmful, deficit panic is. By deflecting the attention of policy-makers from crucial issues, deficit hysteria damages our ability to develop sound economic policy.

Consider jobs. During a recession, the creation of jobs may require the government to stimulate total spending for goods and services. The government can increase total spending by cutting taxes or by increasing its expenditures. But both these actions increase the deficit. Deficit alarm may prevent the government from boosting spending even when it is necessary to put the unemployed to work.

Consider also such urgent social needs as education, worker training, environmental cleanup, health care, research, or the construction of highways and bridges. These needs are not sufficiently profitable to be adequately provided by the private sector. The government must help.[17] Paying for such projects with *current* taxes is often unacceptable, since the benefits of building a bridge or educating a child extend decades into the future. Government borrowing may thus be required in order to spread the cost of such projects over the generations that will benefit.[18] Unfortunately, government borrowing collides with deficit aversion. The result is that crucial social needs may not be met.

Deficit panic causes the media to evaluate proposed economic policies in terms of how much they shrink the deficit. You may read, for example, that President Clinton's budget plan entails a deficit $20 billion greater than the Republican alternative, with no discussion of other aspects of the competing proposals.

Obsession with the deficit diverts attention from issues that really matter: inflation versus unemployment, present versus future consumption, the rich versus the poor. These are the kinds of trade-offs that we *should* evaluate.

8. THE GOALS OF ECONOMIC POLICY

In the climactic weeks of the 1980 presidential campaign, Ronald Reagan asked voters: "Are you better off now than you were four years ago?" The implied answer ("no" for most people) helped Reagan defeat Jimmy Carter.

Suppose that Reagan had asked instead: "Is the United States economy doing better now than it was four years ago?" How could we have answered that broader question? *How can we determine the health of the economy as a whole?*

There is no single index. Economists consider more than one dimension of the economy in order to measure our well-being. In this respect economists are like physicians, who, in evaluating your physical health, look at a variety of indices, such as blood pressure, pulse rate, and weight.

Economists evaluate the health of the economy along three dimensions:

Jobs. The more people are employed, the better is our economic health. One goal of economic policy is to create as many jobs as possible. If employment is pushed too high, however, we generate inflation (a general increase in prices). Inflation is bad. So the government has to balance the benefits of higher employment against the costs of inflation. Weighing these benefits against these costs is a value judgment. In Chapter 2, I examine the relationship between jobs, inflation, and the deficit.

Productivity. Are we producing the things we want? The more the output of goods and services reflects our preferences, the healthier is the economy.

A key distinction is between output that generates current benefits (consumption) and output that creates benefits in the future (investment). (Examples of consumption are food, travel, and entertainment. Examples of investment are machinery, factories, and highways.) The more we sacrifice consumption for investment, the higher the future productivity of our workers and thus our future standard of living. A goal of economic policy is to make the division of output between consumption and investment as close a reflection of our preferences as possible. In Chapter 3, I explore the links between consumption, investment, and the deficit.

Distribution of income. Are we distributing the nation's income between the rich and the poor in accord with our sense of fairness? Do the rich have too much? The poor not enough? A goal of economic policy is to make the gap between the rich and the poor as consistent with our values as possible. In Chapter 4, I discuss the connections between the deficit and the distribution of income.

To evaluate our economic health, all three of these dimensions must be considered. The economy could be seen as doing well on some of these dimensions and not on others. For example, during the 1980s the economy was generating additional jobs at a satisfactory rate without excessive inflation, but productivity growth was widely perceived as too slow. In addition, the gap between the rich and the poor was widening.

9. PLAN OF THE BOOK

In Chapter 1, I look at how American politics has viewed unbalanced budgets from the colonial period to the present. This historical overview reveals that the deficit has traditionally been a powerful negative symbol, signifying different evils in different historical periods.

In Chapters 2, 3, and 4, I examine the relationship between the deficit and the three dimensions of national economic health—jobs, productivity, and the gap between the rich and the poor.

Chapter 5 explores the ominous forecasts for the deficit some decades down the road, along with proposed solutions.

Chapter 6 examines the impending bankruptcy of the Social Security and Medicare trust funds. What does bankruptcy in these trust funds mean, and how do these funds relate to the budget deficit?

Chapter 7 looks at how European countries handle their deficits. I judge their approach to be more reasonable and flexible than ours, but it too has flaws.

Chapter 8 describes the sea change in our national deficit policy that occurred in 1995, when our political leaders decided to aim for a zero deficit rather than a smaller deficit. In this chapter I evaluate the concept of balancing the budget.

Chapter 9 evaluates twelve widely believed myths about the deficit. None of these myths are true, although some are shown to be valid under special circumstances.

In Chapter 10, I provide suggested answers to the questions you are likely to hear when your friends find out you have read this book.

NOTES

1. The "public" includes both the domestic and foreign buyers.

2. The GDP has recently replaced the gross national product (GNP) as the main measure of our national income and output. The GNP is the value of all production by U.S. citizens here and abroad. The GDP includes all production within the United States, whether produced by U.S. citizens or citizens of other countries. The two measures are very similar.

3. For these numbers, see *The Economic and Budget Outlook: Fiscal Years 1997–2006*, May 1996, by the Congressional Budget Office (Washington, D.C.), pp. 15 and 52.

4. The assumption is that the dollar value of our GDP (nominal GDP) will grow at an annual average rate of 5%, which comprises a projected inflation

rate of 3% and a growth rate in our national output (real GDP) of about 2%. See *The Economic and Budget Outlook: Fiscal Years 1997–2006*, May 1996, by the Congressional Budget Office, p. 15. See Chapter 7, Sections 1 and 2, for more discussion of the relationship between the deficit and the public debt.

5. For a summary of the error in this logic, see Chapter 8, Myths 5, 8, and 9.

6. See *The Debt and the Deficit* by Robert Heilbroner and Peter Bernstein, ch. 3. Heilbroner is a professor of economics at the New School of Social Research. Bernstein is a financial analyst who writes for the *Wall Street Journal*.

7. As Heilbroner and Bernstein put it,

National debts serve a very useful purpose: to provide a unique IOU with the full faith and credit of the government behind it. We often forget that government bonds are the only securities that carry such a guarantee of repayment. No state, locality, or corporation can match this guarantee because none of them possesses the powers that put all national governments in a class by themselves—the power to tax their national citizenry . . . and the power to create money. Investors, foreign or national, buy government bonds to do themselves a favor. . . . If we did not have such a gilt-edged debt, we would dearly miss it. (p. 24)

8. For further discussion of this point, see Chapter 8, Myths 1 and 2.

9. The emergence of chronic deficits in the 1970s appears to have been a consequence of two factors: the development of a sense of entitlement to public benefits combined with government miscalculations as to their affordability. The dominant role of the federal government in the Great Depression and the Second World War brought about a shift in what people expected from the government. The appetite for public benefits was whetted. Publicly financed health care and pensions developed strong political support. As our incomes rose, the demand for these benefits increased along with the conviction that the government could afford them. As the sense of entitlement became established, the government ran into unforeseen events that caused spending to climb and revenues to lag. For example, life spans increased, people retired younger, productivity improvement slowed, and the cost of health insurance soared. For a discussion of this hypothesis, see ''Long-Term Tendencies in Budget Deficits and Debt'' by Paul Mason and Michael Mussa in *Budget Deficits and Debt: Issues and Options*, a symposium sponsored by the Federal Reserve Bank of Kansas City, August 31– September 2, 1995, pp. 5–55. Their arguments apply to most industrial countries.

10. *Day of Reckoning* by Benjamin Friedman, p. 4.

11. See *Newsweek*, September 28, 1992.

12. *Facing Up* by Peter Peterson, p. 63. During the 1970s, Peterson served as secretary of commerce and as President Richard Nixon's special assistant for international economic affairs.

13. *The Debt and the Deficit* by Robert Heilbroner and Peter Bernstein, p. 58.

14. *The Misunderstood Economy* by Robert Eisner, p. 3. Eisner is a professor

of economics at Northwestern University, a fellow of the American Academy of Arts and Sciences, and a past president of the American Economic Association.

15. *The Good Society* by John Kenneth Galbraith, p. 53. Galbraith is a professor of economics at Harvard University and is the author of numerous books, including *The Affluent Society, The Culture of Contentment,* and *A Journey through Economic Time.* He is a past president of the American Economic Association and the American Academy of Arts and Letters.

16. The full reasoning here is spelled out in Chapter 3, Section 2. In a nutshell, at high employment, incurring a deficit causes the Federal Reserve to drive up interest rates, which crowds out private investment and increases our indebtedness to foreigners. If the borrowed money is spent on sufficiently productive government investments, our future standard of living will rise. If, on the other hand, the deficit is used for consumption or inferior investments, our future standard of living will fall.

17. For an explanation, see Chapter 3, Section 3.

18. For a discussion, see Chapter 3, Section 4.

1

The Deficit: A Symbol of Evil in American Politics

From the colonial period on, the deficit has been a powerful symbol in American politics.[1] As the political scientist James Savage observed in his detailed history of our attitudes toward the balanced budget:

The American fascination with the idea of balancing the central government's budget is deeply rooted and reflects more than a . . . concern about interest rates, inflation or even the outcome of some recent budget battle.[2]

The deficit has signified a variety of evils, such as a threat to our freedom, our democracy, our Constitution, our equality, our morality, and our children. Dissenting views have appeared from time to time, only to be buried by our overwhelming fear of the deficit.

America's deficit obsession is unique. Even in the nineteenth century our government rejected deficits, while foreign countries freely borrowed.[3] By the time of the Civil War, European countries had debt burdens three to eleven times that of the combined American federal and state governments. In recent decades most European countries as well as Japan have run larger deficits than the United States.[4] Yet budget balancing has not been a central focus of their political debates.[5]

Our traditional view of the deficit as evil has always influenced public policy. Even so, a number of presidents have found reasons to run up huge deficits even while excoriating borrowing. An example is Thomas Jefferson,

1. JEFFERSON AND JACKSON: BALANCING THE
BUDGET TO KEEP GOVERNMENT SMALL

Most American political leaders of the eighteenth and nineteenth centuries shared Thomas Jefferson's view that the public debt was a "mortal cancer."[6] In 1798, Jefferson even suggested in a letter to a friend that a balanced budget amendment be added to the U.S. Constitution.[7] As president, however, he did not pursue that course. In fact, much like President Ronald Reagan, Jefferson overcame his loathing of deficits to incur an enormous increase in the public debt. He believed the national interest was served by borrowing to finance the Louisiana Purchase.[8]

Jefferson's attitude toward debt was rooted in his conviction that deficit spending would encourage manufacturing and bring about an industrial society, as it was doing in England.[9] He distrusted industry because he was appalled at the misery and the inequities that existed in England's urban slums. He believed that freedom and human development flourished best in an agrarian community where independent farmers participated in a republican government. Jefferson also feared that an expanding central government incurring deficits or surpluses would upset the constitutional balance between the federal and state governments and would allow the rich who were holding the public debt to derive unearned profits at the expense of the common laborer. He attached no stigma, however, to borrowing by the state governments.

Jefferson's rival, Alexander Hamilton, had the opposite view. He saw England, with its strong central government, its huge debt, and its industrialized economy, as a positive model. He proclaimed, "A national debt can be to us a national blessing,"[10] and he persuaded many, including George Washington.

Jefferson's view, however, triumphed. As James Savage observed, "After Hamilton met his death at Aaron Burr's hands, many years would pass before anyone argued with such intelligence and conviction about the benefits a public debt and deficit spending might bring to the nation."[11]

Jefferson's belief in states' rights, the avoidance of a strong centralized government, and a balanced budget was passed on and reinforced by President Andrew Jackson and reigned supreme until the Civil War.

As Andrew Jackson expressed it in 1824, the federal debt is a "national curse, [and] my vow [if I become president] shall be to pay the national debt, to prevent a monied aristocracy from growing up around our administration that must bend to its views, and ultimately destroy the liberty of our country.''[12]

2. THE DOMINANT REPUBLICANS: BALANCING THE BUDGET TO EXPAND THE GOVERNMENT

Deficit spending by the federal government skyrocketed during the Civil War. Even in wartime, however, people were frightened by the soaring public debt. President Abraham Lincoln sounded like a modern economist when he tried to assuage public apprehension in his 1864 message to Congress: ''The great advantage of citizens being creditors as well as debtors with relation to the public debt is obvious. Men readily perceive that they can not be much oppressed by a debt which they owe to themselves.''[13]

After the Civil War, unbalanced budgets took on a new significance.[14] Deficits and surpluses were still condemned, but they now signified a lack of administrative efficiency, which connoted unprofessional and dishonest behavior. People felt that as long as the budget was balanced, the federal government would be under public control.

From 1861 until 1932, the dominant Republican Party rejected the Jeffersonian philosophy of a limited federal government. They expanded federal spending but did so in the context of a balanced budget. They increased tariffs (taxes on imports) to raise revenue and to protect domestic industries. Much of the increased revenue they spent on internal improvements, such as harbors and roads, which also benefited their industrial constituency.[15]

The principle of a balanced budget, which had traditionally signified a small federal government, now supported the Republican policy of aiding domestic industry through the expansion of the federal government.

3. THE GREAT DEPRESSION GENERATES REVOLUTIONARY THOUGHTS ABOUT THE DEFICIT

As the economist Herbert Stein observed,

It is impossible to overestimate the importance of the depression as an influence on thinking and policy in the United States over the whole half century from

1930 to 1980. A generation of politicians, economists and general citizens was obsessed by it.[16]

Stein is alluding to the revolution in economic theory that began in the 1930s, brought about by the celebrated British economist John Maynard Keynes. His idea was that deficit spending was needed to pull the economy out of the depression. As a result of this new thinking, the deficit gradually developed a positive as well as a negative face. It still symbolized the presence of the government in the economy, but this presence could now be perceived either as a threat or as a responsible force promoting society's welfare.[17]

President Franklin Roosevelt never wholeheartedly committed himself to Keynes' thinking. The Democrats in Congress were overwhelmingly against deficits. Throughout the Great Depression, Gallup polls, which began in 1935, consistently showed that between 60% and 70% of those interviewed were in favor of balancing the budget even at the cost of cutting government spending. (Sounds like today, doesn't it?) Many in Roosevelt's cabinet supported a balanced budget. His Bureau of the Budget director Lewis Douglas expressed a widely held view when he warned the president that deficits would open the way for fascism or communism in America.[18]

In the 1940s and 1950s, Keynesian economics became the mainstream view of economists. As a result there was a change in political attitudes. Many Democrats and Republicans now embraced the idea that deficits were necessary in a depressed economy. The Employment Act of 1946 reflected the new attitude that the federal government had the responsibility to eliminate unemployment.

President Harry Truman expressed this political orientation by declaring during the recession of 1949, "We cannot expect to achieve a budget surplus in a declining economy. There are economic and social deficits that would be far more serious than a temporary deficit in the federal budget."[19]

President Dwight Eisenhower endorsed this conception of the expanded obligation of government.

Balancing the budget will always remain a goal of my administration. . . . That does not mean to say that you can pick any specific date and say, "Here, all things must give way before a balanced budget." . . . When it becomes clear that the Government has to step in, as far as I am concerned, the full power of Government, of Government credit and of everything the Government has, will move in to see that there is no widespread unemployment and we never again have a repetition of conditions that so many of you here remember when we had unemployment.[20]

Nevertheless, deficits continued to be a powerful symbol of evil. The historian James Sundquist described the image of the deficit during this period.

One cannot read the continuing debates over fiscal policy in the decade prior to 1963 . . . without being impressed with the extent to which the principle of the balanced budget had been not just an economic but a moral percept. The enemies of deficit spending not only attacked deficits as "inflationary," . . . but associated them with patterns of personal conduct that bore a moral stigma—"waste," "profligacy," "recklessness," "spendthrift," " living beyond one's means," "insolvency," and even "immorality."[21]

Keynesian economics reached its peak in American politics in the 1960s and the first half of the 1970s.[22] President John Kennedy was eventually converted to the new economics. He publicly challenged fiscal orthodoxy in his 1962 speech at Yale University.

The myth persists that federal deficits create inflation. . . . Obviously deficits are sometimes dangerous—and so are surpluses. But honest assessment plainly requires a more sophisticated view than the old and automatic cliché that deficits automatically bring inflation.[23]

To stimulate a weak economy, Kennedy proposed a tax reduction in January 1963. He worried about the political fallout from the deficit he was to create, however, and this concern caused him to trim the tax cut recommended by his advisers.

President Richard Nixon was even a more enthusiastic Keynesian than Kennedy. In his State of the Union Message in 1971, he said, "To achieve [a noninflationary recovery], I will submit an expansionary budget this year—one that will help stimulate the economy and thereby open up new job opportunities for millions of Americans."[24]

After the speech, Nixon said in an interview with Howard K. Smith, "Now I am a Keynesian."[25]

In the 1970s the appearance of huge deficits along with simultaneous increases in both inflation and unemployment (stagflation) appeared to discredit the new economics. Beginning around 1975, the acceptance of Keynesian thinking in American politics began to wither. As James Savage sees it, the Democrats needed to defend the virtues of deficit spending "against competing symbolic interpretations of the deficit. Unfortunately for the Democrats, Jimmy Carter proved to be uninterested or unwilling to accomplish this task."[26]

President Carter ignored Keynesian thinking and restored the fixation on reducing the deficit.

I was very concerned in 1976 about the high federal government deficit. When I ran for President, the Federal deficit was over $66 billion. I've not been in office yet two years, but the Congress and I together have already reduced the deficit by $25 billion. I'm now preparing the 1980 fiscal year budget. I'm going to cut the Federal deficit to less than half what it was when I was elected.[27]

By the end of Carter's administration, the Democrats were in disarray about the role deficits should play in fiscal policy.

4. REAGAN AND BEYOND: THE DEFICIT RESUMES ITS EVIL IMAGE

President Ronald Reagan made no attempt to resurrect the notion of a beneficial deficit. His objective was to balance the budget by the end of his first term. In articulating his goal, Reagan drew on the negative deficit associations that had flourished since the earliest period of American history. He accused the Democrats of violating the Constitution by permitting an expanding federal bureaucracy to usurp the rights of the states and to threaten individual freedoms. He also saw deficits as signifying a lack of administrative efficiency. He believed that government spending contained so much fraud and waste that the deficit could be eliminated without cutting government services.[28]

Not only did Reagan perceive deficits as a negative symbol, but he also believed that deficits caused inflation as well as high interest rates. During his first term he changed his mind about these economic effects, since inflation and interest rates were falling at the same time his deficits were soaring. But, when his economic advisers Murray Weidenbaum and William Niskanen stated that deficits were not so worrisome, the Reagan administration hurriedly declared they did care about deficits. As Niskanen later commented, "Once you get closer to Washington, deficits almost become a religious issue, and it's harder to reflect on the issue or even talk intelligently about it."[29]

President Reagan condemned deficits because they symbolized to him a federal government out of control. So, while he was incurring the largest deficits in America's peacetime history, he supported the drive to add a balanced budget amendment to the U.S. Constitution.[30]

Like Jefferson, Reagan tolerated deficits because he believed the national interest required them. To him, the deficits were not as bad as surrendering his tax cut or his escalation in military spending. Moreover, he asserted that raising taxes to eliminate the deficit wouldn't work. It would simply cause the government to boost its spending.[31]

In the 1980s and 1990s, Keynesian thinking has become a negligible factor in the American political dialogue, though it remains the mainstream view of professional economists.[32] From President Carter through President Clinton, there has been scarcely a mention of any benefits of federal borrowing, even in a depressed economy.[33] The traditional symbol of the deficit as evil has triumphed in the wake of the record-breaking Reagan and Bush deficits.

From Reagan to the present, deficits symbolize to many Americans an inability to govern ourselves.[34] Both the Republicans and the Democrats have rejected federal borrowing for any reason. Contrary views are feeble cries in the political wilderness. As Democratic congressman Leon Panetta (President Clinton's former budget director and chief of staff) expressed in 1981, "Like a rose, a deficit is a deficit is a deficit."[35]

In the following chapter, I argue that under certain conditions deficit spending is necessary to eliminate unemployment and that our historical aversion to deficits has frequently led to the destruction of jobs and lost output.

NOTES

1. For a historical view of the deficit, see *Balanced Budgets and American Politics* by James Savage and *Deficit Government* by Iwan Morgan. For a more technical historical approach, see "History, Analytics and Accounting, Analogies of the Debt," in *Debt and the Twin Deficits Debate*, edited by James Rock, pp. 7–29.

2. *Balanced Budgets and American Politics* by James Savage, p. 3.

3. Ibid, p. 86.

4. Ibid., pp. 2–3. Larger, that is, in relation to the size of their economies, more specifically, the deficit as a percentage of their GDP.

5. I suspect that one reason other countries don't panic over deficits as do we is that their budgets—unlike ours—are typically constituted on the sound accounting principle of distinguishing current from capital expenditures. Consequently, their deficits are incurred for the purpose of financing public invest-

ments, which generate future assets. By contrast, our federal budget is a mishmash of current expenses as well as investment; thus there is no way to link our deficits with the creation of future assets. For a discussion of this point, see *The Debt and the Deficit* by Robert Heilbroner and Peter Bernstein, pp. 93–97, The *Misunderstood Economy* by Robert Eisner, pp. 93–94, and this book, Chapter 3, Section 4.

6. *Deficit Government* by Iwan Morgan, p. 8.

7. *Balanced Budgets and American Politics* by James Savage, p. 106.

8. *Debt and Taxes* by John Makin and Norman Ornstein, p. 6.

9. *Balanced Budgets and American Politics* by James Savage, ch. 4.

10. *Debt and Taxes* by John Makin and Norman Ornstein, p. 6.

11. *Balanced Budgets and American Politics* by James Savage, p. 97.

12. Ibid., p. 104, and "History, Analytics and Accounting Analogies of the Debt" in *Debt and the Twin Deficits Debate*, edited by James Rock, p. 10.

13. "History, Analytics and Accounting, Analogies of the Debt" in *Debt and the Twin Deficits Debate*, edited by James Rock, p. 11.

14. *Deficit Government* by Iwan Morgan, pp. 4–9, and *Balanced Budgets and American Politics* by James Savage, ch. 5.

15. *Balanced Budgets and American Politics* by James Savage, p. 136.

16. *Presidential Economics* by Herbert Stein, p. 29.

17. *Balanced Budgets and American Politics* by James Savage, p. 174.

18. *Deficit Government* by Iwan Morgan, p. 28.

19. Ibid., p. 79.

20. *Balanced Budgets and American Politics* by James Savage, p. 175.

21. *Politics and Policy: The Eisenhower, Kennedy, and Johnson Years* by James Sundquist, pp. 46–47.

22. A new symbol emerged to represent the new economics. This symbol was the "full-employment budget," that is, the budget according to economists' estimates of what government spending and revenues would be if the economy were operating at full employment. A deficit at less than full employment could be estimated to be a balanced budget or even a surplus at full employment, since a stronger economy generates more taxes. The goal, according to Keynesian thinking, was to balance the full-employment budget rather than the actual budget. As the full-employment budget became the accepted focus, the federal government was granted political elbow room, or a heat shield, to engage in deficit spending in a depressed economy.

23. *Balanced Budgets and American Politics* by James Savage, p. 177.

24. *Presidential Economics* by Herbert Stein, pp. 172–173.

25. Ibid

26. *Balanced Budgets and American Politics* by James Savage, pp. 186–187.

27. Ibid., p. 191.

28. Ibid., pp. 202–203.

29. Ibid., p. 210, and *Presidential Economics* by Herbert Stein, p. 274.

30. *Debt and Taxes* by John Makin and Norman Ornstein, p. 182.

31. *Balanced Budgets and American Politics* by James Savage, pp. 214–215.

32. See the following chapter for evidence on this point.

33. An exception is President Clinton's failed attempt to pass a modest stimulus package in the spring of 1993. See Section 9 of the following chapter.

34. *Debt and Taxes* by John Makin and Norman Ornstein, p. 3.

35. *Balanced Budgets and American Politics* by James Savage, p. 225.

2

Jobs, Inflation, and the Deficit

1. CREATING JOBS

Suppose you lose your job. Who do you blame? Yourself? The firm that fired you? The government? The culprit could be any of these. But since the Great Depression of the 1930s, *economists have come to understand that the economy may not automatically generate enough jobs. The government must help.* We learned this lesson the hard way: throughout the decade of the 1930s, between 14% and 25% of the workforce was idled.

The view of mainstream economists is that the major cure for unemployment is to boost total demand (total spending on goods and services).[1] Total demand includes spending by consumers, businesses, the government, and foreigners. If spending from any of these sources increases, businesses will experience an increase in the demand for their products. They will react by stepping up production, thus creating more jobs.

To understand why this is so, imagine that you are a manufacturer of, say, T-shirts. For some reason people start buying more T-shirts. Your sales increase, and your inventory of shirts shrinks. Since you are in business to earn profits, you will respond, if you can, by gearing up production to satisfy the higher demand and to replenish your depleted inventory. More production requires more workers. More workers mean more employment.

These same relationships hold for the economy as a whole: as demand increases, employment increases.

What role should the government play in curing unemployment? *The government must see to it that total demand is increased.* How can the government do this? It could increase its own spending or stimulate private spending by reducing taxes.[2]

As Paul Samuelson and William Nordhaus put it in their famous text:

Recessions and unemployment are often caused by insufficient aggregate (total) demand. When this is so, government policies that successfully augment demand—such as increases in government spending—can be an effective way to increase output and reduce unemployment.[3]

But here's the rub: increasing government spending or cutting taxes enlarges the deficit. If the country is suffering from deficit phobia, the government may not have access to these remedies. Furthermore, there is sometimes no other cure for unemployment. An aversion to deficits may prevent the government from responding appropriately to high levels of unemployment.

Consider the recession that began in mid-1990. By early 1992, many economists had come to believe that the economy was not going to recover quickly unless the government boosted total demand by deliberately increasing the deficit. Reflecting this judgment was an open letter written in March 1992 and sent to President Bush, members of Congress, and Federal Reserve chairman Alan Greenspan. The letter was signed by dozens of distinguished economists, including six Nobel Prize winners:

the Congress should enact and the President should sign a program of additional federal assistance to state and local governments amounting to at least $50 billion a year. . . . The spending of these funds will help to stimulate the economy. Since the economy has idle resources of labor and capital available to meet additional spending with additional production and the threat of inflation is minimal, it is appropriate to let these expenditures add to the deficit financed by borrowing, and it would cancel most or all of the needed stimulus to aggregate demand if they were financed otherwise.[4]

Deficit panic prevented our government from following these economists' advice. Unemployment remained high for over two more years.

As a more dramatic example, consider the Great Depression of the 1930s. At that time, neither politicians nor economists understood that unemployment could be cured by cutting taxes or increasing government spending.[5] To make matters worse, deficits were considered evil. The Roosevelt administration felt pressured by public opinion to eliminate the tiny deficits that were being incurred.

Listen to President Roosevelt in 1937:

I have said fifty times that the budget will be balanced for the fiscal year 1938. If you want me to say it again, I will say it either once or fifty times more. That is my intention.[6]

Roosevelt fulfilled his pledge. He cut the deficit in 1938 by trimming government spending and raising taxes. The impact was disastrous. The economy, which had recovered somewhat by 1937, plunged deeper into the depression during 1938. Burned by this outcome, Roosevelt began to accept deficit spending as a necessary therapy for joblessness. But he acted on too small a scale. The depression hung on.

As James Savage has described it:

Accepting deficits did not come easily to Franklin Roosevelt, who as a presidential candidate dedicated himself to restoring balanced federal budgets. Consequently, though Roosevelt eventually came to accept deficit spending, his deficits during those crucial New Deal years of 1933–1940 never climbed above $4.4 billion.[7]

What cured the Great Depression? The skyrocketing deficit spending of World War II! During the war, military spending went through the roof and, along with it, the deficit. Federal expenditures rose from $9.0 billion in 1939 to $95.6 billion in 1944, while the deficit soared from over $2 billion to over $54 billion. As a result unemployment vanished. The rate of unemployment fell from 17.2% in 1939 to under 1.2% in 1944. What a tragedy that it took a world war to cure the Great Depression.

2. JOBS VERSUS INFLATION

Many fear that increasing total spending will trigger inflation. This fear is well founded if unemployment is low.

Consider again your T-shirt firm. Imagine that your output capacity is 1,500 T-shirts a day; that is, you could produce 1,500 shirts per day if your plant were operating at full capacity. Suppose further that you are

currently selling 1,500 T-shirts a day. What if the demand increases to
1,800 T-shirts a day? You will most likely raise your price and sell at a
larger profit. Since you are not able to expand production, an increase
in demand will push up your price.

Unlike a single factory, the entire economy rarely operates at full
capacity. T-shirt factories may be producing around the clock, while
dress-shirt factories have idle capacity. For this reason, a general increase
in demand almost always has a twofold effect when employment is high:
it not only creates new jobs but also causes inflation. The T-shirt pro-
ducers will boost prices, while the dress-shirt industry will put people to
work.

Consider 1987, a year of high employment. From 1987 to 1989, total
spending (GDP) climbed from about $4.7 trillion to $5.4 trillion, spurred
by deficit spending.[8] As a result, unemployment dropped from 6.2% to
5.3% and inflation rose from 3.6% to 4.8%.[9]

By contrast, consider what happens when total demand increases while
unemployment is high. During a recession your T-shirt firm might be
able to sell only a fraction of its output capacity, say 700 T-shirts a day.
Imagine now that demand increases to 900 shirts a day. You will be
happy to produce more because you have unused capacity. Will you also
raise prices? Probably not. You would be afraid to be undersold by your
hungry competitors, who also have unused capacity during a recession.

The same reasoning holds for the economy as a whole. *When unemployment is high, an increase in total demand will create jobs but is
unlikely to boost inflation.*[10] During 1983, the economy was suffering
from a severe recession, with an unemployment rate of 9.6%.[11] From
1983 to 1986, total demand (GDP) increased by almost a trillion dollars,
fueled by the soaring deficits that were incurred under President Reagan.
The unemployment rate fell to 7.0% with no increase in inflation.

*In an economy plagued by joblessness, boosting total spending will
put people to work. Increasing spending may require a larger deficit.
The higher is employment, the greater the risk that additional spending
will be inflationary. In a high employment economy, the benefit of additional jobs must be balanced against the damage resulting from higher
inflation.*[12]

When employment is high, the government faces a painful choice.
Should it push up spending, generating more jobs but causing more inflation? Politicians differ in how they weigh the benefits of jobs against
the costs of inflation. Pushing up total spending involves winners and

losers. There is no scientific way of measuring the losers' pain against the winners' pleasure.

Economists can't tell you how you *should* balance jobs against inflation (although some talk as if they can). That is a value judgment that you, the voter, must make.

3. WHAT'S SO BAD ABOUT INFLATION?

Inflation redistributes income. Suppose that inflation is occurring at a rate of 3% per year; that is, the average price level is increasing by 3%. If your income is also rising by 3%, you are neither hurt nor helped by inflation. If your income rises by less than 3%, you are hurt. If it rises by more, you are helped. Inflation robs some, while it gives others a windfall. One reason inflation is so despised is that the victims are selected capriciously.

Consider senior citizens trying to scrape by on pensions. They were lenders to pension funds in the 1950s or 1960s, expecting to be paid back with interest when they retired. Since prices have risen more than expected in the meantime, they are being paid back in less valuable dollars than anticipated. On the other hand, anyone who borrowed to buy a house in the 1950s or 1960s experienced a bonanza due to inflation. They have been paying off their mortgage in cheaper and cheaper dollars.[13]

More generally, lenders and borrowers fare differently under inflation. Suppose you have lent me money, and we agreed that I will pay you $100 a month for x months. Normally, we will have built into our agreement a certain anticipated rate of inflation. If inflation is higher than expected, which of us is hurt? You are. The $100 you receive each month buys less than anticipated. I, on the other hand, am helped. I'm giving you dollars worth less than expected. Unexpected inflation hurts lenders and benefits borrowers.

Inflation also creates uncertainty by causing price patterns to change. This confusion hurts us.[14]

Suppose you go to your favorite supermarket and find that prices are suddenly higher. What do you do? Do you dish out the extra money and worry that you are being ripped off? Or do you shop around? Either way you bear a cost.

Inflation may also cause you to rethink your purchases and your work schedule. Can you still take that vacation, buy that VCR, or turn down that extra job? More headaches.

A similar logic applies to firms: they may now be forced to use some of their workers to compare suppliers or recalculate budgets, workers whose time could have been spent doing something more productive.

4. HOW DOES THE GOVERNMENT REGULATE TOTAL SPENDING?

When unemployment is high, the government should stimulate total demand. But how? It can use either *monetary policy* or *fiscal policy*.

Monetary policy is conducted by our central bank, the Federal Reserve System (the Fed), not by the Congress or the president. The Fed is, in effect, a fourth branch of government. It is the most powerful financial institution in the country.

What does the Fed do? If you have wondered about that, you're in good company. President Reagan was puzzled too. Shortly after his inauguration in January 1981, he met with Paul Volcker, who had been chairman of the Fed since his appointment by Jimmy Carter in 1979.[15] Lou Cannon gives this account of the meeting in his biography of Reagan:

Three days after his inauguration, Reagan had startled the Secret Service by walking out the front door of the White House and down Pennsylvania Avenue to the Treasury Building, where he lunched with Volcker. Aides who attended the lunch would never forget it. Reagan was barely seated before he said to the chairman, ''I was wondering if you could help with a question that's often put to me. I've had several letters from people who raise the question of why we need any Federal Reserve at all. They seem to feel that it is the Fed that causes much of our monetary problems and that we would be better off if we abolished it. Why do we need the Federal Reserve?'' Martin Anderson [a Reagan aide] sitting directly across from Volcker observed that ''his face muscles went slack and his lower jaw literally sagged a half-inch or so as his mouth fell open. For several seconds he just looked at Reagan, stunned and speechless.'' . . .

Volcker, however, recovered quickly from his surprise, and gave a good account of himself. . . . He then lectured Reagan briefly on the Fed's role. . . . His answer apparently satisfied the President, who never raised the question again.[16]

Chairman Volcker undoubtedly informed President Reagan that the *major task of the Fed is to regulate total spending. It does so by driving interest rates up or down.*[17]

A reduction in interest rates stimulates spending. Lower interest rates reduce the cost of borrowing, thus stimulating borrowing and spending. A decline in interest rates encourages purchases of new homes and autos and other consumer durables, as well as business investment in factories and equipment.[18]

A monetary policy that stimulates spending by lowering interest rates is called an *easy money policy*; the reverse, a *tight money policy*.

When Paul Volcker became chairman of the Fed, inflation was our main economic problem, thanks to the soaring price of imported oil. The inflation rate in 1979 was over 11% a year and climbing.[19] Volcker proclaimed that inflation was public enemy number one and said that he would fight it with the strongest measures. He instituted a tight money policy. Interest rates were pushed higher and higher through 1981, reaching the highest levels in modern times. For example, the three-month Treasury bill rate, 7.2% in 1978, rose to over 10% in 1979, 11.5% in 1980, and 14% in 1981.[20]

The result was the recession that President Reagan inherited and that worsened during the first two years of his tenure. The unemployment rate soared from 5.8% in 1979 to 9.7% in 1982. The recession did, however, break the back of inflation, lowering it from 13.3% in 1979 to 3.8% in 1982.[21]

By the spring of 1982, unemployment and bankruptcies were higher than at any time since the Great Depression. It seemed as if the recession was never going to end. A tight money policy was appearing less and less defensible. Finally, in mid-1982, Fed chairman Volcker switched to an easy money policy. As a result, the three-month Treasury bill rate dropped from 12.1% in June 1982 to 8.0% in December of that year, moving down to under 6% in 1986.[22]

Volcker's sharp reversal of monetary policy helped generate the economic upswing that began in 1983.

President Reagan's fiscal policy helped. *Fiscal policy* refers to government expenditures and tax rates. A fiscal policy that boosts total demand is called a *fiscal stimulus*. The reverse is a *fiscal contraction*.

Ronald Reagan's policy provided a fiscal stimulus: he increased government spending and reduced tax rates.

Reagan did not present his spending policy as a way of putting people to work. He talked in terms of beefing up our military spending in order to counteract the "evil empire" (the Soviet Union). He more than doubled defense spending from 1980 to 1987, increasing it from $134 billion to $282 billion.[23] This spending increase constituted a boost in total demand, since it consisted of purchases of goods and services. Reagan also presided over a huge increase in *transfer payments*, that is, outright grants, such as Social Security and Medicare. These expenditures increased from $291.8 billion to $471.1 billion over this period.[24] Higher transfer payments increase total demand because the recipients have more purchasing power. *Total* government spending—purchases plus transfer payments—increased sharply: from $590.9 billion in 1980 to $1,003.9 trillion in 1987.[25]

President Reagan's tax policy was the other facet of his fiscal stimulus. Reagan saw taxes as strangling the economy. He pushed through a reduction in personal income tax rates of 25%, 5% in 1981 and 10% in each of the following two years. Like transfer payments, tax cuts stimulate total spending by increasing after-tax income.[26]

Ronald Reagan's program of increasing government spending and reducing tax rates delivered a walloping fiscal stimulus to a stagnant economy. His policy contributed to the longest peacetime boom in our history, beginning in 1983 and lasting to mid-1990. Eighteen million new jobs were created, while inflation remained modest.[27]

A necessary consequence of a fiscal stimulus is an expansion in the deficit (or a reduction in the surplus). Had the increase in government spending been matched by a comparable increase in taxes in order to avoid swelling the deficit, the fiscal stimulus would have been negligible. Under Reagan, the federal deficit increased from $79.0 billion in 1981 to $149.8 billion in 1987.[28] *The soaring deficit helped power the economic upswing.*

5. MONETARY VERSUS FISCAL POLICY

How is it best to increase total spending, with monetary policy or fiscal policy or both?

The Fed can change monetary policy on a dime. Changing fiscal policy may take a long time, since the president and the Congress need to thrash out legislation. As a result, policy to alter total demand is usually carried out by the Fed.

On the other hand, *monetary policy has more limited power to regulate total demand than does fiscal policy.* Interest rates can be pushed down only so far and can boost total spending only by so much. Fiscal policy can, in principle, supply as much stimulus to total demand as needed. Monetary policy has been likened to a scalpel; fiscal policy, to a meat ax. Thus, the conventional wisdom: *a fiscal stimulus should be invoked only in special circumstances, such as a severe recession that persists in spite of an easy money policy.* This view was reflected in the economists' open letter of March 1992:

The protracted weakness of the economy since 1989 signals unusual risks that monetary measures alone cannot produce a timely and healthy recovery. That is why it is prudent to adopt fiscal measures to help get the economy moving this year.[29]

6. STRUCTURAL VERSUS AUTOMATIC DEFICITS

Listening to the media, you would think that deficits are always a bad thing, that the goal in good and bad times alike should be to balance the budget. It may come as a surprise, then, to learn that there is at least one type of deficit that all economists agree is a good thing, namely, the *automatic (cyclical) deficit.*

To understand the automatic deficit, consider what happens when you lose your job. Your income shrinks. Your tax payments shrink as well. This reduction occurs automatically. Congress doesn't have to pass a new law.

In addition, you become eligible for benefits. You may receive transfer payments such as unemployment compensation, Medicaid, or food stamps. These benefits are automatically available assuming you satisfy the eligibility requirements.

In other words, the government automatically softens the blow of unemployment by decreasing your taxes and increasing your benefits. Your purchasing power is thereby enhanced, bolstering your spending.

When the economy falls into a recession, millions lose their jobs. With no change in the law, the resulting reduction in tax revenues and increase in transfer payments move the budget into a deficit. This is the *automatic deficit.* It not only helps individuals but combats the recession by stimulating total spending. Because an automatic deficit serves to cushion the decline in employment, it is also called an *automatic or built-in stabilizer.*

Economists admire this characteristic of our economic system, that is, that the deficit automatically increases whenever the economy slumps. Here is what the text of Paul Samuelson and William Nordhaus has to say about this type of deficit:

the modern economy is blessed with important "built-in stabilizers." Requiring no discretionary action, tax receipts change automatically when income changes. . . . The same stabilizing effect is produced by unemployment compensation and other welfare transfers that grow automatically as income falls.[30]

In the recession brought on by Volcker's tight money policy from 1979 to 1982, the automatic deficit grew by $75.3 billion.[31] It has been estimated that for every percentage-point increase in our unemployment rate, the deficit is automatically increased by about $40 billion.[32]

Economists distinguish the automatic deficit from the *structural deficit*.[33] The structural deficit is defined as *the deficit that would exist if the economy were at full employment*, given the existing tax laws and eligibility requirements for entitlements.[34] The structural deficit, by definition, is not affected by fluctuations in the unemployment rate.

The actual deficit is the sum of the structural deficit and the automatic deficit.[35] For example, suppose the deficit is $300 billion at an unemployment rate of 7.5%. Assume that an unemployment rate of 5.5% is taken to be full employment. If the deficit automatically declines by $40 billion for every percentage-point reduction in the unemployment rate, the structural deficit would in this case be $220 billion, and the automatic deficit would be $80 billion.

Changes in fiscal policy imply changes in the structural deficit. If the government institutes a fiscal stimulus by boosting its spending or reducing tax rates, the structural deficit is increased. Conversely, if the government carries out a fiscal contraction by cutting its spending or increasing tax rates, the structural deficit is decreased. *Changes in the structural deficit are thus taken to be a measure of the thrust of fiscal policy*.[36]

Consider, for example, the fiscal stimulus that took place under President Reagan. The structural deficit increased from $46.7 billion in 1982 to $184.7 billion in 1986.[37] The automatic deficit, on the other hand, declined by $54 billion during this boom period.

This relationship between the two types of deficit is typical: a rise in the structural deficit will, by driving up national income, reduce the automatic deficit. *Statistical studies show, however, that a fiscal stimulus increases the structural deficit by more than it decreases the automatic deficit*. Therefore, a fiscal stimulus expands the actual deficit.[38] The reverse is also true: a fiscal contraction reduces the actual deficit because it diminishes the structural deficit by more than it expands the automatic deficit.

Politicians and the media condemn deficits without distinguishing between those that are automatic and those that are structural. Alarm bells go off even when the growing deficit is protecting us from the ravages of a deteriorating economy. In the recession of 1981–1982, for example, the soaring deficit was almost entirely automatic.[39] Nevertheless, President Reagan felt the political heat.

Lou Cannon observed that the deficit "became the Reagan administration's principal albatross."[40] Herb Stein, an economic adviser to the Reagan administration, described how the workings of the automatic stabilizer during 1981–1982 caused all hell to break loose:

By December (1981) . . . economic conditions had deteriorated. . . . And word was leaking out of the administration that the deficits for the next few years would run around $100 billion a year. This was shocking news. . . . The administration seemed unable to make up its mind about how to respond . . . a member of the Council of Economic Advisors (to Reagan), William Niskanen, offered a number of reasons for not being worried about the deficits. . . . This appearance of insouciance caused consternation and the administration hurried to say that . . . deficits were bad after all. . . . There began a period of negotiation, name-calling and struggle between the President and the Congress, the House and the Senate, the Republicans and Democrats. . . . The object of all this activity was first to avoid responsibility for the deficits and second to reduce the deficits.[41]

What a shame that the Reagan administration felt that the public was too naive to understand that this automatic deficit was a blessing, that without it even more jobs would have been lost.

Amazingly, in the middle of this deep recession, the Democrats proposed higher taxes in order to trim the deficit. In April 1982, Congressman Daniel Rostenkowski, Democratic chairman of the House Ways and Means Committee, proposed raising taxes by $35 billion for fiscal 1983. It was common knowledge that such a fiscal contraction would likely worsen the recession.

President Reagan resisted these pressures. He clung to his conviction that taxes should be kept down and that military spending should rise. Consequently, the deficit continued to escalate. From 1982 to 1986, the deficit soared from $128 billion to $221 billion.[42] This deficit increase, however, was not the built-in stabilizer. It was Reagan's fiscal stimulus, reflected in jumps in the structural deficit. His policy energized the recovery. The unemployment rate fell from almost 10% in 1982 to 7% in 1986.[43]

The media's reaction to the expanding deficit was hysteria. On March 5, 1984, *Time's* cover featured the headline "That Monster Deficit— America's Economic Black Hole" with a picture of a black hole sucking in dollars. The article quotes Chrysler Chairman Lee Iacocca saying, "It is a scandal, I don't know what they're on down in Washington. It's wacko time." A survey of 1,000 registered voters conducted for *Time* found that 64% considered the deficit a major issue and that 23% regarded it as the most serious problem facing the United States.

In the 1984 presidential election, Democratic candidate Walter Mondale made the deficit his main charge against President Reagan, even though unemployment was still high. Mondale's economic agenda proposed a fiscal contraction: increasing taxes and cutting government spending in order to slash the deficit.

The president's reaction to such attacks was vintage Reagan. To *Newsweek* he boasted that he had cut taxes, restored America's military might, eliminated needless federal regulation of business, and pruned wasteful domestic spending. So what if he hadn't fulfilled his pledge to balance the budget by 1984? As he put it, "I've succeeded in four of those five goals. I'm batting 800 and that's pretty good in any league I know about."[44]

By contrast to the media and the politicians, the reaction of most economists to the surge in the deficit in the first half of the 1980s was favorable. Here is the evaluation in the text of William Baumol and Alan Blinder:

In 1981–1982, the economy went through a deep recession. And in 1983, the first year of the recovery, unemployment was still far above its full employment level. Under these circumstances, crowding out would not be expected to be a serious problem and actions to close the deficit would have threatened the recovery. According to the basic principles of fiscal policy, a large deficit was probably appropriate.[45]

The Harvard economist Benjamin Friedman, in his book *The Day of Reckoning*, argues passionately against large chronic deficits. But here is what he has to say about the growing deficit from 1982 through 1984:

By the end of 1984, just two years into the recovery, business activity overall had grown by an impressive 11% . . . and four million fewer workers were unemployed. The Reagan recovery was well under way. And not despite the deficit but *because* of it. The increased spending and reduced taxes that ran up more than $400 billion in accumulated deficits during just the three fiscal years 1982–84 were the same increased spending and the same reduced taxes that spurred the business recovery.[46]

The prevailing view of economists is that the growing deficits during the first half of the 1980s were a good thing.[47] In 1981–1982, increases in the deficit resulted from the automatic stabilizers, which diminished the severity of that downturn. From 1982 to 1986, the increases in the deficit reflected a fiscal stimulus that fueled the recovery from a serious recession.

When considering employment, economists are more interested in the structural deficit than in the deficit itself. Changes in the structural deficit are a measure of the thrust of fiscal policy. The actual deficit, on the other hand, implies nothing about jobs or inflation or fiscal policy. It is a hodgepodge, reflecting a mixture of cyclical and policy influences.

As the text of Paul Samuelson and William Nordhaus expressed it:

By distinguishing cyclical (automatic) deficits from structural deficits, we get a better reading of the true impact of fiscal policy. To gauge the impact of fiscal policy, it is necessary to watch the structural budget. If the actual deficit increases in a given year, one might be tempted to say, ''The deficit is up, therefore the government is stimulating the economy.'' But this assessment could be dead wrong.[48]

If the automatic deficit is a good thing, what about the structural deficit? Is it good or bad? It depends. Increasing the structural deficit during a severe recession such as the one that occurred in 1982 *could* be an unmixed blessing. On the other hand, a fiscal stimulus in a high employment economy usually generates both benefits and costs: more jobs, on one hand, but also more inflation.

7. DEFICITS IN A RECESSION

Most economists agree that if the economy is in a slump that the Fed is unable to cure, then the deficit should be deliberately increased; that is, the structural deficit should be boosted. Such a fiscal stimulus, by increasing total spending, will create jobs and alleviate poverty. Moreover, inflation will not be triggered as long as the deficit increase is not excessive, as illustrated by the Reagan upswing of 1982–1986.

Furthermore, as far as creating jobs is concerned, it doesn't matter what the additional spending is on! As the great economist John Maynard Keynes argued, it is better to hire people even to build pyramids or dig up dollar bills buried by the government than to leave them unemployed.[49] When workers receive income for their labor, they will spend more on goods and services, thus generating additional jobs and income, which causes additional spending, and so on. Income will therefore rise by a multiple of the initial spending increase. The spending fans out and benefits everyone.

But some of you may be asking, Don't deficits push up interest rates? A deficit requires the Treasury to sell securities to the public. Doesn't this borrowing drive up interest rates?

This reasoning is correct as far as it goes. But it ignores the dominant role of the Federal Reserve. *The Fed has the last word on interest rates.*[50] In a recession, the Fed will be pushing interest rates down because it wants to encourage borrowing and spending. For example, in the recovery from the recession of 1982, the deficit grew, while interest rates declined. The same pattern characterized the sluggish period of 1990–1993.

8. DEFICITS AND INTEREST RATES AT HIGH EMPLOYMENT

Increasing the structural deficit during periods of high employment is another matter. Under these conditions, a fiscal stimulus will cause the Fed to drive up interest rates. Fearing inflation, the Fed will attempt to prevent a surge in total demand. If the resulting tight money policy succeeds, the increase in the structural deficit will not cause inflation.

The Fed has traditionally been our chief guardian against inflation. The Fed chairman and the other members of the Board of Governors are typically drawn from banking and financial circles. As such, they tend to be lenders, and remember, inflation hurts lenders.[51] To the Fed, preventing inflation is the main goal of monetary policy.

This attitude is reflected in the response of Fed chairman Paul Volcker when asked about the suffering resulting from his tight money policy in the early 1980s, a policy that decreased the inflation rate from about 10% to 4% at the cost of pushing over 6 million people under the poverty line:

Yeah, I know, hurting the poor. . . . You help the *rentier* class and you hurt the workingman. . . . You have to start with the conviction that price stability is better than inflation and that "better" means better for economic growth and stability and in the long run better for everybody. High or low interest rates aren't ends in themselves.[52]

As the current Fed chairman Alan Greenspan put it:

the most productive function the central bank can perform is to achieve and maintain price stability.[53]

Jobs and poverty have not enjoyed as high a priority with the Fed as preventing inflation. This is not to deny that the Fed's policy-makers have lowered interest rates during recessions. They have.[54] But inflation has been their main worry. For example, while the Federal Reserve Bank Act of 1978 requires the Fed to pursue full employment as well as low inflation, Chairman Greenspan has publicly said he favors changing the law so that price stability will be the Fed's sole objective.[55]

Central bankers from around the world attending a conference at Jackson Hole, Wyoming, in November 1994 raised an uproar when Alan Blinder, newly appointed by President Clinton to the Federal Reserve Board, argued that the Fed should give employment and inflation equal priority. As the British journal *The Economist* described the scene:

Unemployment . . . according to the latest conventional wisdom is not something for which central bankers are responsible. Instead, it is argued, monetary policy should be focused exclusively on low inflation. Sharp intakes of breath could therefore be heard around the room when Alan Blinder, the newish vice-chairman of America's Federal Reserve Board, insisted that central banks could use interest rates to reduce unemployment. . . . Mr. Blinder had directly contradicted Alan Greenspan, the Fed's chairman.[56]

When the Congress and the president initiate a fiscal stimulus (an increase in the structural deficit), and the Fed reacts by raising interest rates, these branches of government appear to be working at cross purposes. In fact, *the Fed is attempting to crowd out private spending to make room for the additional spending generated by the fiscal stimulus.* This notion of *crowding out* is important, so bear with me. At high employment, a fiscal stimulus will likely be inflationary. By driving up interest rates, the Fed hopes to prevent this inflation. Higher interest rates depress consumer spending on durables and business spending on factories and equipment. Thus, a tight money policy crowds out private spending.[57] If the Fed is successful in keeping a lid on *total* spending, the upshot of the fiscal stimulus is that the crowded-out spending is replaced by the additional government spending and the increased spending caused by the tax cut. If the Fed is unsuccessful, however, the fiscal stimulus may cause inflation as well as higher interest rates.

Consider, for example, the Vietnam War period of the late 1960s. The economy was at high employment. By early 1966 President Lyndon Johnson's advisers were urging a tax increase sufficient to prevent the escalating war spending from triggering inflation. The president resisted. Consequently, the structural deficit jumped.[58]

By 1966, the inflation rate had increased by more than 1.5 percentage points. Fed chairman William McChesney Martin reacted by driving up interest rates. The three-month Treasury bill rate, which was under 4% in 1965, reached 6.7% by 1969. In spite of rising interest rates, total demand surged.[59] Chairman Martin's tight money policy had not succeeded in crowding out enough private spending to make room for the additional military spending. As a result, the inflation rate escalated from 1.9% in 1965 to 6.2% in 1969.[60]

Employment was also high during the last two Reagan years, 1987–1988. Nevertheless, his fiscal stimulus continued, due to rising defense spending and entitlements. The structural deficit jumped from $118.9 billion in 1987 to $151.2 billion in 1988.[61]

In 1987 President Reagan replaced Paul Volcker with Alan Greenspan as chairman of the Federal Reserve System. Greenspan immediately tightened monetary policy to cool down the economy. The three-month Treasury bill rate rose from 5.8% in 1987 to 8.1% by December 1988.[62] In this case, the Fed succeeded in crowding out enough private spending to contain the inflation rate, which stabilized at about 4.5% during 1987–1989.[63]

Is an increase in the structural deficit at high employment good or bad? Such a policy involves both costs and benefits, so your answer depends on your values. In pondering the question, you might consider the following issues:

- The increased deficit, along with higher interest rates, implies higher interest payments to the holders of the public debt. You and your children will be taxed to meet these interest payments. Will the interest payments on the debt rise faster than your income over the long run? The answer hinges on the nature of the deficit spending. I discuss this issue in Chapter 3.

- How much do you value the output caused by the fiscal stimulus relative to the output crowded out by the tight money policy? President Reagan incurred deficits by increasing spending on such items as defense, Social Security, and Medicare. The Fed responded by raising interest rates, causing a reduction in spending on autos, housing, factories, and equipment. Was the expanded output resulting from the growth in defense, Social Security, and Medicare more or less "valuable" than the cutback in the production of autos, housing, factories, and equipment? There is no "right" answer to this question. You might ask yourself, though, whether the crowded-out spending would have done more than the deficit spending to increase your standard of living and that of your children. I explore this question in Chapter 3.

- What impact will an increase in the deficit and the accompanying tight money policy have on the rich versus the poor? This depends on how the fiscal stimulus is carried out—whose taxes are lowered, whose entitlements are increased, who benefits from the government purchases. I examine the relationship between deficits and the gap between the rich and the poor in Chapter 4.

- What if the Fed fails to prevent an increase in total spending? The increase in the structural deficit may be large enough to overwhelm the tight money policy, as happened during the Vietnam War. In this case, there could be an additional cost: inflation. There may also be an additional benefit: even at high employment an increase in total demand usually creates jobs.

9. DEFICIT AVERSION AND JOBS

In 1936, the celebrated British economist John Maynard Keynes published *The General Theory of Employment, Interest and Money*. The book was a bombshell—the most revolutionary contribution to economics of the twentieth century. One of my professors who had been a graduate student at Harvard when Keynes' book appeared told me that after studying it he and his classmates were "in a daze for the next two years." Economists who studied Keynes at that time could never view the economy the same way again. They had long believed that depressions cured themselves and that deficit spending did not increase employment but only crowded out private spending. Keynes persuaded economists that deficit spending created jobs. Responding to the notion that, in the long run, depressions cure themselves, Keynes replied, "In the long-run we are all dead."

By the end of World War II, a revolution had taken place in economic theory. Keynesian economics—the idea that recessions could be cured by deficit spending—had become conventional wisdom among econo-

mists. *It still is.* In a 1992 survey of more than 400 professional economists employed in the United States, 91% agreed that raising
government spending or lowering tax rates is an effective way to increase
employment.[64]

*In spite of this consensus our aversion to deficits has repeatedly
caused the destruction of jobs.*

Dwight Eisenhower was the first president who consciously followed
Keynesian thinking. During the downturn of 1958, he boosted government spending, which resulted in a $12.8 billion deficit in 1959, an
enormous deficit for that period.[65] Eisenhower's fiscal stimulus turned
the tide. The unemployment rate declined by 1.3 percentage points from
1958 to 1959.

Then as now, however, many perceived the deficit as the embodiment
of evil. It's not surprising, then, that Eisenhower shied away from deficits
in his last two budgets. Despite warnings from his economic advisers,
Eisenhower was determined to balance the budget and even leave a surplus as he left office.[66] He reduced the structural deficit by almost $12
billion from 1959 to 1960. His contractionary fiscal policy helped push
the economy back into a slump. The unemployment rate rose from 5.5%
in 1959 to 6.7% in 1961.[67] Richard Nixon believed that he lost the election to John Kennedy in 1960 because of Eisenhower's determination to
erase the deficit. The upshot was that President Kennedy inherited an
economy in recession.

While I was a graduate student at the University of Michigan, some
of my professors served as advisers to President Kennedy. They boasted
that they were "teaching economics to the president," and they admired
how apt a student he was. According to one story, Kennedy was on his
yacht with several economists, and one of them was regaling him with
a long-winded explanation of how a fiscal stimulus creates jobs. Another
interrupted saying, "You don't have to explain that to Jack. He took that
course." Kennedy shot back: "Shhhh. Let him explain. I got a C in it."

According to George Ball, undersecretary of state from 1961 to 1966:

he [Kennedy] well understood the teachings of John Maynard Keynes as inter-
preted to him by Walter Heller, James Tobin, and Paul Samuelson. Keynes
thought that a President should use fiscal policy to try to maintain a robust
economy approaching full employment. If that required deficits, . . . no matter.[68]

Under this influence President Kennedy decided to counter the Eisenhower recession with a fiscal stimulus. He selected an across-the-board

tax cut. As I heard it, Kennedy instructed his economic advisers to compute how big a tax reduction would be required to create as much employment as possible without inflation. When they brought him their calculations, he surprised them by asking, "How big a deficit will this tax reduction create?" When they told him, he asked, "Is that deficit bigger than Eisenhower's?" When they said yes, he ordered them to decrease the tax cut so that the deficit would not exceed Eisenhower's. Kennedy's economists argued with him. They were confident that their recommended tax reduction would not be inflationary. They pointed out that a smaller tax cut would generate fewer jobs. The president was unshakable. He was convinced that exceeding Eisenhower's deficit would be politically damaging.[69] He said to his economists, "Why the hell don't you guys teach economics so I don't keep running into this anti-deficit flak?"

As a result of the huge Reagan deficits of the 1980s, alarm over deficits has worsened. Nowadays, deficit panic rules out the use of fiscal policy to cure unemployment. Worse, the relentless pressure to balance the budget implies a continuously contractionary fiscal policy. The burden of counteracting this drag on the economy rests with the Fed.

In January 1989, President Ronald Reagan bequeathed a full employment economy to George Bush. In addition, inflation had been tamed. Even the deficit had been declining, falling from 5.1% of GDP in 1986 to 3.1% in 1988.[70] In his economic report upon leaving office, Reagan said:

Today, it is as if the world were born anew. . . . We have unleashed the creative genius of ordinary Americans and ushered in an unparalleled period of peacetime prosperity.[71]

Reflecting the deficit hysteria, President Bush sounded a very different note in his inaugural address:

our funds are low. We have a deficit to bring down. We have more will than wallet. . . . We will make the hard choices.[72]

As Herb Stein, economic adviser to Presidents Nixon and Reagan, observed:

George Bush was the prisoner of his inheritance. He inherited a large budget deficit. . . .[73] The idea that our funds were low and that we had more will than

wallet reflected a common attitude at the time. The notion that America was a
poor country, unable to meet its needs . . . was not that the country was poor,
which it was not, but that the government was poor, as evidenced by its deficit.[74]

In Bush's first year in office, fiscal policy became contractionary, helping to push the economy into a slump.[75] Even with the weak economy
President Bush and the Congress agreed to a five-year, $500-billion def-
icit-reduction program. This package of spending cuts and tax increases
guaranteed that fiscal policy would remain contractionary.

In spite of the declining interest rates brought about by Fed chairman
Alan Greenspan, the economy stagnated from 1990 through 1993. During this period, many economists urged a fiscal stimulus, as is evident
in the open letter quoted before in Sections 1 and 5, but their advice was
drowned out by cries for deficit reduction. One of the Nobel Prize-
winning economists signing the open letter was Robert Solow. He argued
against deficit reduction in testimony before the Joint Economic Committee of the Congress:

Deficit reduction will be contractionary for the economy. That is why the Fed
is needed to take up some of that slack. It would be a terrible mistake, I think,
to impose that . . . contractionary force at a time when the economy is just strug-
gling to emerge from a very deep recession.[76]

In the spring of 1993, President Clinton tried to pass a small stimulus
package. Again, the deficit was a stumbling block. As the *New York
Times* reported on April 21, 1993, the day Clinton's proposal was defeated:

On the winning side Senator Dole quietly argued that Republicans, too, want
jobs. But asserting that ''a fundamental difference of philosophy has brought us
to this point,'' the Kansas Senator said his party viewed the plan as too expensive and fatally flawed because it added to the deficit instead of having its
spending matched by cuts elsewhere in the budget.

As Senator Dole undoubtedly knew, if the additional spending *had*
been matched by spending cuts elsewhere, there would have been no
increase in total demand and no reason to expect job creation.

Economists have estimated that the sluggish recovery from the recession of 1990 cost us around 3.5 million jobs over the two-year period
beginning in March 1991.[77] As George Kahn, an economist at the Federal

Reserve Bank of Kansas City, said, "While a 'typical' recovery would have produced 4.3 million jobs in its first eight quarters, the current recovery has produced fewer than 900,000."[78] Kahn pointed out that a major cause of the anemic creation of jobs was insufficient total spending. Had we not been obsessed with bringing down the deficit, we could have used fiscal policy to increase employment during this stagnant period.

I fear that deficit aversion will continue to slow the rate at which our economy creates jobs. President Clinton's economic advisers gave him the same warning. In his book *The Agenda*, Bob Woodward described one of the presidential briefings given by the economist Alan Blinder, then a member of Clinton's Council of Economic Advisors:

Clinton asked about job creation. Would they get the 8 million new jobs he had promised?

The contraction caused by deficit reduction could cost several million of those jobs, Blinder said. Only lower interest rates could offset the loss. . . .

The effect on Clinton was electric. The dangers of the emerging deficit reduction package seemed clearer. "If we do all this and bleed all over the floor, and Greenspan doesn't help," he said, "we're screwed."[79]

But the deficit reduction bandwagon was too powerful to resist. As Woodward reports:

[Labor secretary] Robert Reich listened carefully to the [President's 1992 State of the Union] speech from the House floor. He saw for himself the great tidal wave of deficit reduction that had been pounding at Clinton. All the freshmen congressmen, mostly New Democrats, conditioned by the Ross Perot summer, were talking only about the deficit. Any time somebody leaned over to tell Clinton to be bold, they really meant to be bold about deficit cutting. (pp. 139–140)

"If you could feel the mood on the Hill, Mr. President," [Budget Director Leon] Panetta said. . . . They all had grossly underestimated the . . . power of Perot's deficit reduction message. . . . (p. 163)

the White House staff were being bombarded by members of Congress, and the cry was always the same: More deficit reduction. (p. 229)[80]

As the economists Dean Baker and Todd Schafer observed:

discussion of the deficit in policy circles has reached a level of unreality that is extraordinary even for Washington. Ostensibly intelligent and responsible individuals are talking about ''stimulating the economy'' by reducing the deficit. . . . The fact that deficit reduction is contractionary . . . seem(s) to have disappeared from the discussion. The conventional wisdom on deficit reduction has come to be the more the better, and the sooner the better.[81]

In August 1993, President Clinton, like President Bush, negotiated a more than $400-billion, five-year, deficit-reduction plan with Congress involving tax increases and spending cuts. Here is what the 1993 Report of the Joint Economic Committee of the Congress said about the 1993 budget agreement:

President Clinton's deficit reduction plan will continue to exert downward pressure on economic activity.[82]

If continuous deficit cutting does create a chronically sluggish economy, is that all bad? As usual, there is a flip side: a slack economy may be a less inflationary economy. So, if inflation hurts you more than recession, deficit aversion could work in your favor. This could be true, for example, if you are retired on a fixed income.

10. MISMEASURING THE DEFICIT

As Robert Eisner has pointed out, during periods of inflation conventional measures of the deficit exaggerate its size.[83] As a result, our political leaders have sometimes succumbed to deficit panic when the budget was actually running a surplus! While Eisner's reasoning is endorsed by his fellow economists, it has yet to show up in our political debates.

Consider how inflation affects the deficit. Recall that the deficit is defined as the increase in the public debt over a certain time period, usually a year. During inflation, the rising price level erodes the *real* value—that is, the purchasing power—of the public debt. Thus, while government borrowing adds to the public debt, a rising price level over the same time period diminishes the real value of the debt. The official deficit includes only the effect on the public debt of borrowing but not the effect of inflation. For example, suppose the government borrows $100 billion, increasing the public debt from $500 billion to $600 billion over a given year. The official deficit would weigh in at $100 billion.

Now, suppose the average price level rose by 4% during that year. The $600 billion of debt at the end of the year would have lost 4% of its purchasing power, or about $24 billion.[84] The *real* increase in the public debt is not $100 billion; it is only about $76 billion. The official deficit would overstate the *real deficit* by about $24 billion.

Let's look at this same point from another angle. The deficit is also defined as the excess of government spending over taxes. The conventional measure of the deficit includes interest on the debt as just another form of government spending. While that treatment seems natural, it overstates spending and hence the deficit whenever prices are rising. Since inflation shrinks the government's indebtedness, part of the interest on the public debt merely restores the real value of the government securities. That part of the interest should therefore not be counted as government spending and included in the deficit. In our example, $24 billion of the interest received by holders of the public debt is not *real interest*; it is only a compensation for the loss in the purchasing power of government securities.[85] The official deficit overstates the real deficit by counting this $24 billion as government spending and therefore as part of the deficit. One implication of this mismeasurement is that a balanced budget is, in reality, a budget surplus, except under the unlikely conditions of zero inflation.

Another adjustment that should be made in measuring the deficit is the inclusion of state and local governments.[86] One reason for federal deficits is the large amounts the federal government has given to the state and local governments in the form of *grants-in-aid*, which have enabled these governments to run substantial surpluses, exceeding $85 billion annually in the past decade.[87] The combined deficits of all levels of government have therefore been considerably smaller than the deficits of the federal government. Since the deficit is a measure of government borrowing from the private sector, the relevant deficit is the combined deficit, not just the federal deficit.

A striking example of policy reacting to a false deficit signal occurred in the administration of President Jimmy Carter. Due mostly to oil price increases and bad harvests, inflation soared at the end of the 1970s. At the same time the official budget deficits were huge. Conventional wisdom held that the deficits were causing the inflation.[88] The political pressures to balance the budget escalated. Twenty-nine states approved a constitutional amendment to balance the budget, and 81% of respondents to the Gallup poll approved such an amendment.

President Carter was also convinced that the deficits were the culprit.[89]

As he wrote in his memoirs, "the threat of rising inflation and budget deficits preyed on my mind."[90] His economic advisers questioned the president's conviction that the price increases were caused by the deficit. In response to the question of whether deficit spending in the late 1970s was responsible for the inflation, Charles Schultze, the chairman of the Council of Economic Advisors under Carter, replied, "Only moderately. Only a little. I think it was principally, not solely, oil prices in 79–80, and food prices in 78."[91]

This deficit hysteria caused budget cuts that helped create the deepest recession since the 1930s. Unemployment increased by over 2 million from 1979 to 1981.[92] As James Savage sees it,

If Carter's aides had serious doubts that the FY 1979 budget . . . was creating double-digit inflation . . . they apparently made little effort to convince Carter to adopt their way of thinking. For in response to the perceived relationship between deficits and inflation, the administration submitted a restrictive FY 1980 budget to Congress. . . . The budget proposal included a $3.1 billion cut in Comprehensive Employment and Training Act (CETA) training programs, a $2.6 billion reduction in health care funds, and a $600 million proposed drop in social security.[93]

The tragic irony is that a correct deficit measure would have revealed that the federal budget was not incurring deficits at all. It was, in fact, running surpluses! Moreover, state and local governments, thanks to the federal government, were also in surplus. Consider 1980.[94] The publicly held federal debt was about $700 billion, and the inflation rate was about 10%. Thus, about $70 billion of federal spending was compensating for the erosion in the value of the public debt. The official deficit of $74 billion consisted, therefore, of a *real* deficit of only $4 billion. In addition, the automatic (cyclical) deficit was $17 billion. Hence, the federal budget really had a structural surplus of $13 billion. Moreover, state and local governments were receiving over $80 billion of grants-in-aid from the federal government and were consequently running surpluses of over $50 billion. Similar calculations hold for 1978 and 1979.[95]

Another example of fiscal policy responding to a misleading measure of the deficit occurred under President George Bush in the full-employment year of fiscal 1989. The official federal deficit was $152 billion.[96] One of Bush's main priorities was to bring down this "huge" deficit. He consequently instituted a contractionary fiscal policy, helping to trigger the stagnation of the early 1990s.[97] The public debt in 1989 was $2.1 trillion, and the inflation rate was 4.1%. Hence, around $86 billion (4.1% of $2.1 trillion) of federal spending restored the lost purchasing power of the public debt. Using this inflation adjustment, the federal deficit was not $152 billion; it was really only $66 billion. Moreover, state and local governments were running a surplus of over $95 billion that year, with over $118 billion of their revenues coming from the federal government in grants-in-aid. Therefore, the combined budget of all levels of government was about $30 billion in surplus in 1989! Yet, President Bush in his inaugural lamented that ''we have a deficit to bring down and we have more will than wallet,''[98] and he led the crusade to reduce the deficit.

One more adjustment ought to be made in measuring the deficit, one that many economists believe is crucial, that is, subtracting from the deficit government borrowing for the purpose of creating long-lived assets, referred to as public investment.[99] As with a household or a business or a state or local government, such borrowing hardly qualifies as a ''deficit'' since the incurred debt is offset by a future asset.

Robert Eisner estimates public investment for fiscal 1989 to be around $70 billion. Subtracting his figure of $70 billion along with the inflation adjustment of $87 billion from the official 1989 federal budget deficit of $152 billion yields a federal budget surplus of $5 billion. By these calculations, President Reagan bequeathed President Bush a tiny federal surplus rather than a huge deficit.

In the following chapter, I explore the relationship between investment, the long-run rate of increase in our standard of living, and the deficit.

NOTES

1. For evidence, see a survey of economists in the *American Economic Review*, May 1992, p. 20. To the statement, ''Fiscal policy (e.g., tax cut and/or expenditure increase) has a significant stimulative impact on a less than fully-employed economy,'' 59.3% of those surveyed generally agreed, 30.6% agreed with provisos, and 9.1% generally disagreed.

Two types of unemployment are resistant to an increase in total spending: frictional unemployment and structural unemployment. Frictional employment consists of people who are between jobs. It is, for the most part, voluntary. Structural unemployment is made up of people who don't have the required skills to hold a job. Diminishing structural unemployment would involve long-run programs of education and training, in addition to adequate total spending.

Because of frictional and structural unemployment, it is unrealistic to aim for an unemployment rate of zero.

2. Another way for the government to increase spending is to lower interest rates. See Section 4 of this chapter.

3. *Economics* by Paul Samuelson and William Nordhaus, 14th ed., p. 576.

4. *Challenge*, March–April 1992, p. 64.

5. The idea that deficit spending can cure a depression was developed by the British economist John Maynard Keynes in his *General Theory of Employment, Interest and Money*, published in 1936. For more on Keynes, see Section 9 of this chapter.

6. *Balanced Budgets and American Politics* by James Savage, p. 170.

7. Ibid., p. 169. As Savage also points out, Roosevelt's enemies "saw deficits as a threat to democracy and a stimulus to totalitarian government . . . and the government's deficits provided them with a convenient issue in attacking the Democratic programs and the president" (p. 173).

8. *Economic Report of the President*, February 1996, p. 280.

9. Ibid., pp. 324, 347.

10. This point is made in the open letter by the six Nobel laureates quoted in the previous section.

11. For the data in this paragraph, see the *Economic Report of the President*, February 1996, pp. 280, 324.

12. Many people worry that inflation could start to accelerate; that is, prices could start rising at faster and faster rates. For an economy like ours, this possibility is remote. As Alan Blinder said in *Hard Heads, Soft Hearts*, p. 51, "There is neither theoretical nor statistical support for the popular notion that inflation has a built-in tendency to accelerate."

13. See, for example, *Economics* by William Baumol and Alan Blinder, 7th ed., ch. 23.

14. This confusion is exacerbated by the evidence from research that increasing inflation implies greater volatility in prices.

15. Paul Volcker had previously served as undersecretary for monetary affairs in the Nixon administration and subsequently became chairman of the Federal Reserve Bank of New York. He was succeeded as chairman of the Fed by Alan Greenspan in 1987.

16. *President Reagan—The Role of a Lifetime* by Lou Cannon, p. 268.

17. The main way the Fed pushes interest rates down is by purchasing government securities from the public. The public winds up with less securities but a larger supply of money (mostly checking and savings deposits). Increasing the supply of anything lowers its price. Interest rates are the price of money. Reversing this process drives interest rates up. For an introduction to monetary policy, see *Economics Explained* by Robert Heilbroner and Lester Thurow, ch. 10, 11; or *Memos to the President* by Charles Schultze, Memos 16 and 17.

18. In addition, monetary policy affects total demand via the exchange rate:

a reduction in U.S. interest rates cheapens our dollar relative to foreign currencies, thus stimulating exports and discouraging imports. This chain of effects is discussed in the next chapter.

19. *Economic Report of the President*, February 1996, p. 347.

20. Ibid., p. 360.

21. Ibid., pp. 324, 348. For an examination of the enormous costs involved in bringing down inflation by causing unemployment and poverty, see *Hard Heads, Soft Hearts* by Alan Blinder, ch. 2.

22. For monthly data on interest rates, see various issues of the *Federal Reserve Bulletin*, Board of Governors of the Federal Reserve System.

23. *Economic Report of the President*, February 1996, p. 369.

24. *The Economic and Budget Outlook: Fiscal Years 1997–2006*, Congress of the United States, Congressional Budget Office, May 1996, p. 138. These transfer payments are labeled "Entitlements and Other Mandatory Spending."

25. *Economic Report of the President*, February 1996, p. 367.

26. See *Day of Reckoning* by Benjamin Friedman, ch. 10.

27. *Economic Report of the President*, February 1996, pp. 319, 347.

28. *The Economic and Budget Outlook: Fiscal Years 1997–2006*, Congress of the United States, Congressional Budget Office, May 1996, p. 134.

29. *Challenge*, March–April 1992, p. 64.

30. *Economics*, 14th ed., by Paul Samuelson and William Nordhaus, p. 625. See also *Memos to the President* by Charles L. Schultze, p. 205.

31. Computed from *The Economic and Budget Outlook: Fiscal Years 1997– 2006*, Congress of the United States, Congressional Budget Office, May 1996, pp. 133–134.

32. *Economics*, 14th ed., by Paul Samuelson and William Nordhaus, p. 627.

33. Also called a *standardized-employment* or *high-employment* deficit.

34. "Full employment" is currently considered by the Congressional Budget Office (CBO) to be employment that would exist at an unemployment rate of 5.5%. This rate, which is an educated guess, is determined as the lowest unemployment rate that can be achieved without generating excessive inflation.

35. This was the definition I used to compute the increase in the automatic deficit from 1979 to 1982 from *The Economic and Budget Outlook: Fiscal Years 1997–2006*, Congress of the United States, Congressional Budget Office, May 1996, pp. 133–134. In 1979, the CBO calculated the deficit to be $40.7 billion and the structural (standardized-employment) deficit as $52 billion, implying that the automatic deficit was in surplus, equal to $11.3 billion. In 1982, the deficit was $128 billion, and the structural deficit was $64 billion; hence, the automatic deficit was $64 billion. It follows that the automatic deficit increased by $75.3 billion from 1979 to 1982.

36. A change in the structural deficit is only a rough measure of the impact of fiscal policy. This is true because different types of government spending and taxes affect spending differently. For example, a decrease in taxes on million-

aires will increase spending less than an equal decrease in taxes on the poor, although both would imply the same increase in the structural deficit. Economists have developed more sophisticated measures of fiscal stimulus and contraction, measures that take into account the different total spending implications of various government expenditures and taxes. See, for example, *The 1993 Joint Economic Report* of the Joint Economic Committee of the Congress of the United States, April 1, 1993, p. 51.

37. These calculations of the structural and automatic deficits are by the CBO. See *The Economic and Budget Outlook: Fiscal Years 1994–1998*, Congress of the United States, Congressional Budget Office, January 1993, p. 123.

38. *Economics*, 14th ed., by Paul Samuelson and William Nordhaus, p. 625.

39. *The Economic and Budget Outlook: Fiscal Years 1994–1998*, January 1993, pp. 123–124. The deficit increased from $79 billion to $128 billion from 1981 to 1982, while the structural deficit rose only from $37.4 billion to $46.7 billion.

40. *Ronald Reagan—Role of a Lifetime* by Lou Cannon, p. 246.

41. *Presidential Economics* by Herb Stein, pp. 274, 275.

42. *The Economic and Budget Outlook: Fiscal Years 1997–2006*, Congress of the United States, Congressional Budget Office, May 1996, p. 134.

43. *Economic Report of the President*, February 1996, p. 325.

44. *The Deficit and the Public Interest* by Joseph White and Aaron Wildavsky, p. 386.

45. *Economics*, 7th ed., by William Baumol and Alan Blinder, p. 766.

46. *Day of Reckoning* by Benjamin Friedman, pp. 139–140.

47. This is not to say there was agreement as to the nature of the tax reductions or the additional government spending. This subject is dealt with in the following chapters.

48. *Economics*, 14th ed., by Paul Samuelson and William Nordhaus, p. 625.

49. See *John Maynard Keynes—the Economist as Savior 1920–1937* by Robert Skidelsky, pp. 554–555.

50. See Section 4 in this chapter.

51. See Section 3.

52. See the interview with Paul Volcker in *Audacity*, Fall 1994, p. 9.

53. Testimony before the Subcommittee on Economic Growth and Credit Formation of the Committee on Banking, Finance and Urban Affairs of the U.S. House of Representatives, July 20, 1993, appearing in *Challenge*, September–October 1993, pp. 4–10.

54. For evidence that the Fed has typically fought recessions, see "What Ends Recessions?" by Christina Romer and David Romer, National Bureau of Economic Research Working Paper No. 4765.

55. *The Economist*, September 3, 1994, p. 78.

56. Ibid.

57. There is an additional effect, which I examine in the next chapter. An

increase in U.S. interest rates increases the value of the dollar, which reduces our net exports and thus decreases the total demand for our output.

58. The structural deficit increased by $30 billion from 1965 to 1968. It would have increased more except that inflation during this period automatically pushed people into higher tax brackets and thus increased tax revenues. ''Bracket creep'' was eliminated in 1985.

59. Total spending increased from $703 billion in 1965 to $960 billion in 1969.

60. In 1968, President Johnson finally proposed a tax increase. After months of bitter debate, a temporary tax increase was passed by Congress. Thus, in 1969 fiscal policy turned contractionary, and the inflation rate came down in 1970 and again in 1971. See *Presidential Economics* by Herb Stein, pp. 118–122.

61. The structural deficit fell from 1986 to 1987, but more sophisticated measures indicate that there were a small fiscal stimulus in 1987 and a larger one in 1988. See the *1993 Joint Economic Report, April 1, 1993*, p. 52.

62. For monthly data on interest rates, see various issues of the *Federal Reserve Bulletin*, Board of Governors of the Federal Reserve System.

63. *Economic Report of the President*, February 1996, p. 348.

64. See ''Is There a Consensus among Economists in the 1990s?'' by R. M. Alston, J. R. Kearl, and M. B. Vaughan in the *American Economic Review*, May 1992, pp. 204–205.

65. *Balanced Budgets and American Politics* by James D. Savage, p. 175.

66. Ibid., p. 176.

67. *Economic Report of the President*, February 1996, p. 324.

68. *The New York Review of Books*, February 3, 1994, p. 20.

69. Ibid.

70. *The Economic and Budget Outlook: Fiscal Years 1997–2006*, Congress of the United States, Congressional Budget Office, May 1996, p. 135.

71. *Presidential Economics* by Herb Stein, p. 413.

72. Ibid., p. 417.

73. Ibid., p. 427.

74. Ibid., p. 418.

75. See *The 1993 Joint Economic Report* of the Joint Economic Committee of the Congress of the United States, April 1, 1993, pp. 49, 53.

76. Ibid., p. 56.

77. See the ''Clinton Budget Package: Putting Deficit Reduction First?'' by Dean Baker and Todd Schafer in *Challenge*, May–June 1993, p. 6.

78. See ''Sluggish Job Growth: Is Rising Productivity or an Anemic Recovery to Blame?'' in the *Economic Review* of the Federal Reserve Bank of Kansas City, Third Quarter 1993, pp. 5–19.

79. *The Agenda* by Bob Woodward, pp. 85, 95.

80. Ibid, pp. 139–140, 163, 229.

81. *Challenge*, May/June 1993, p. 4.

82. See the *Report of the Joint Economic Committee* of the Congress of the United States, April 1, 1993, p. 53. This quote is from the Democratic side of the committee.

83. See *Economics*, 7th ed., by William Baumol and Alan Blinder, pp. 752–754 and *The Debt and the Deficit* by Robert Heilbroner and Peter Bernstein, ch. 7. For a more advanced analysis, see *How Real Is the Federal Deficit?* by Robert Eisner, ch. 2.

84. More precisely, the real value of the debt at the end of the year would be $600 billion divided by price index of 1.04, which is about $576.92 billion. Thus, the loss in value is $23.08 billion.

85. If the average interest rate on government securities were, say, 7%, the interest payment would be $42 billion. The *real interest rate* earned by holders of the public debt would, however, be less than 7% due to the inflation, assumed here to be occurring at 4% a year. The real interest rate would be $42 billion minus $24, or $18 billion, as a percentage of $600, or about 3%. The real interest rate is the market rate less the inflation rate.

86. See *Economics*, 7th ed., by William Baumol and Alan Blinder, p. 755.

87. See the *Economic Report of the President*, February 1996, p. 374. Since 1993, the annual surpluses of state and local governments have exceeded $90 billion.

88. See "Measuring the Deficit" by Robert Eisner in *Debt and the Twin Deficits Debate*, edited by James Rock, p. 83.

89. *Balanced Budgets and American Politics* by James Savage, pp. 186–195.

90. Ibid., p. 192.

91. Ibid.

92. Civilian unemployment was 6.137 million in 1979 and 8.273 million in 1981. See the *Economic Report of the President*, February 1996, p. 318.

93. *Balanced Budgets and American Politics* by James Savage, pp. 192–193.

94. For the calculations for 1980, see "Measuring the Deficit" by Robert Eisner in *Debt and the Twin Deficits Debate*, edited by James Rock, pp. 83–84. See also The *Economic and Budget Outlook: Fiscal Years 1997–2006* by the CBO, May 1996, pp. 133–134.

95. These calculations convert the official federal deficits of around $40 billion in 1979 and $60 billion in 1978 to federal surpluses of $24 billion and $7 billion, respectively. Moreover, both in 1978 and 1979, state and local budgets were running surpluses of over $50 billion. Cyclical deficits in both 1978 and 1979 were negligible. For the federal debt figures, see *The Economic and Budget Outlook: Fiscal Years 1997–2006* by the CBO, May 1996, p. 134. For the inflation numbers and the state and local surpluses, see the *Economic Report of the President*, February 1996, pp. 348 and 274, respectively.

96. These 1989 calculations are in "Measuring the Deficit" by Robert Eisner in *Debt and the Twin Deficits Debate*, edited by James Rock, pp. 83–84.

97. See the previous section for a discussion of this recession.

98. *Presidential Economics* by Herb Stein, p. 417.

99. See, for example, *The Debt and the Deficit* by Robert Heilbroner and Peter Bernstein, pp. 81–85; *How Real Is the Federal Deficit* by Robert Eisner, pp. 30, 179; and *Economics*, 7th ed., by William Baumol and Alan Blinder, p. 755.

3

The Deficit and Our
Future Standard of Living

1. PRODUCTIVITY

Most of us want more than a job. We want some assurance that our income and our standard of living will rise over the years. Only improvements in productivity can raise the average standard of living over the long run. (A higher standard of living doesn't necessarily imply another car or a bigger television. It could mean better health or a cleaner environment or less crime.[1])

As MIT professor Paul Krugman put it:

Productivity isn't everything, but in the long run it is almost everything. A country's ability to improve its standard of living over time depends almost entirely on its ability to raise its output per worker.[2]

Or listen to Alice Rivlin, the first director of the CBO and current director of the Office of Management and Budget (OMB):

It is hard to overestimate the importance of productivity growth to the economic future of Americans. Unless the population is spending more time working, the level of living can rise only if workers produce more goods and services per hour of work. . . . Hence, a crucial ingredient of a brighter economic future is making productivity grow faster.[3]

If productivity stalls, incomes stagnate. In the United States, incomes have been stagnating since 1973. From 1947 to 1973, our incomes grew quickly because productivity was increasing rapidly. During that period, both output per worker and median family income (adjusted for inflation) grew by almost 3% a year, fast enough to double the standard of living in 25 years. The main causes of this surge in productivity were education, modernization of the workplace, and improved technology.[4]

Since 1973, productivity and median income have risen by less than 1% a year. At this rate it would take 80 years to achieve the same increase in standard of living that was achieved in less than a generation following World War II. This productivity slowdown is a key fact about our economy in the past 25 years.[5] The remedy is clear: the nation must increase the quantity and quality of *investment*.

Economists divide spending into two categories: investment and consumption. *Investment is spending designed to enhance the future productivity of the labor force.* It includes spending on tools, machinery, highways, bridges, airports, worker training, research, and improvements in technology. In contrast to investment, which is future-oriented, consumption yields its benefits now. It is not intended to improve future worker productivity. We consume when we spend on food, clothes, entertainment, gifts, and vacations.

Here is what Alice Rivlin says about improving productivity:

A slew of study groups . . . have addressed this question. . . . Most prescriptions call for drastic improvements in education and training. . . . Another common theme . . . is the need to improve public infrastructure.[6]

During his 1992 campaign for the presidency, Bill Clinton pledged to carry out these policy recommendations. He proposed to increase federal spending on new technology, worker training, children's health, and infrastructure. As president, Clinton has frequently referred to these *public investment* projects as "the things I got elected for."

During 1993, many of Clinton's proposed investments were eviscerated by the deficit-reduction craze. Some were lopped off by the spending caps (ceilings on discretionary spending[7]) that were built into President Bush's five-year budget agreement of 1990.[8] Bob Woodward reports that Clinton was shocked and enraged when he discovered what these caps were doing to his economic program:

Slamming his fist down on the end of his chair, Clinton let loose a torrent of rage and frustration. He said he felt blindsided. . . . Why hadn't they ever had a serious discussion about the caps? . . . Why didn't they tell me? he asked. This is what I was elected for, he said. This is why I'm here. . . . "We have just gone too far. We're losing our soul."[9]

As Woodward tells it, budget director Leon Panetta explained to the president that when he had tried to get the spending caps raised to spare Clinton's investments, he had run into the brick wall of deficit phobia.[10]

The reporter Elizabeth Drew tells a similar story:

the President was upset that the Congress was cutting back his "investments." He complained that his staff hadn't adequately explained to him the extent to which the "caps" on domestic appropriations limited new spending. . . . Clinton complained in one meeting, "Maybe there's nothing we can do, but I sure would feel better about this if we really had understood how difficult the caps were, (so) that we would have had a strategy to get deficit reduction and investment and meet the caps."[11]

Clinton's investment program came under further attack when the non-partisan Congressional Budget Office (CBO), under the direction of Robert Reischauer, projected that deficit reduction was going to fall $60 billion short of the president's stated goal. Pouncing on this news, the House chopped spending by another $60 billion, much of the money coming out of Clinton's proposed investments. President Clinton reportedly reacted to this setback by saying, "We've gutted our investment program by turning the government over to Reischauer!"[12]

Bob Woodward described this conflict between deficit reduction and public investment by saying, "The fault line between the deficit hawks and the [public] investment hawks, once just a hairline fissure, now cracked open."[13]

If public investment hawks like Clinton wanted to enhance labor productivity, what did the deficit hawks want? Why were they so determined to cut the deficit? Must we choose between deficit hawks and investment hawks?

2. DEFICIT HAWKS

A deficit incurred during a period of high employment crowds out private investment, thus lowering our children's standard of living. This was the battle cry of the deficit hawks. Recall that crowding out occurs because the Fed boosts interest rates to prevent deficit spending from boosting total spending and causing inflation. (Put differently, the deficit

absorbs savings that would otherwise be channeled into private investment.) Conversely, reducing a deficit (or increasing a surplus) brings
down interest rates, which stimulates (crowds in) private investment,
thereby improving our future standard of living.

In addition, the deficit hawks point out that *deficits cause foreign indebtedness, which puts another drain on the income of future generations.* Why should deficits increase foreign indebtedness? As the Fed
raises interest rates in response to the deficit, our securities become more
attractive to foreigners. To purchase our securities, foreigners buy dollars, which drives up the value of the dollar relative to foreign currencies.[14] An increase in the value of our dollar cheapens our imports and
makes our exports more expensive to foreigners. Consequently, our exports fall, and our imports rise. An excess of imports over exports is
called a *trade deficit.* How do we pay for an excess of imports? By
borrowing from foreigners, that is, by sending them assets. Thus, a trade
deficit increases our indebtedness to foreigners.

*According to the deficit hawks, then, reducing a deficit (or increasing
a surplus) boosts our children's standard of living in three ways: private
investment is stimulated, our debt to foreigners is reduced, and the future
taxes necessary to pay interest on the public debt are lowered.* The cost
of these future benefits is that the *current* generation has to tighten its
belt, since cutting a deficit, or boosting a surplus, means higher taxes
and/or reduced government spending.

Many economists have argued that we should eliminate chronic deficits. One of the most impassioned is the respected Harvard economist
Benjamin Friedman:

The chronic federal deficit is sapping our productivity at home and our ability
to compete abroad. As a result, our standard of living has already begun to grow
more slowly, and America's influence in world affairs has suffered.[15]

Nobel laureate Paul Samuelson also embraces this view:

The proximate cause of the chronic . . . [trade] deficits . . . is the new devil in
American life—the basic structural federal deficit. . . . The evil of a basic structural deficit is that it is the devil's recipe for a low-saving economy.[16]

Another distinguished deficit hawk is Alice Rivlin:

If the government were borrowing less . . . more resources would be available for private investment to increase future productivity. Therefore elimination of the federal budget deficit would make a crucial contribution to income growth.[17]

Finally, listen to the columnist Hobart Rowen:

Of all the self-inflicted wounds of the past three decades, none has been more harmful than the public debt saddled on the American people by the eight years of Reaganomics. . . . There has been an actual decline in real weekly U.S. earnings from $315 in 1972 (in 1992 dollars) to a mere $255 in October 1992—a drop of almost 20%. As a result many American families had to turn to more than one breadwinner . . . from 1978 through 1991 real median family income showed no change, despite the increase in hours worked.[18]

Are the deficit hawks right? Will reducing the deficit (or increasing the surplus) increase our future standard of living? Their argument is correct—as far as it goes.

What the deficit hawks fail to point out is that *our future standard of living depends not only on private investment, foreign indebtedness, and future taxes. It also depends on public investment.* Public investment can also enhance future productivity.

Deficit hawks assume, often implicitly, that in cutting the deficit we will cut government spending on consumption (e.g., Social Security and Medicare).[19] If that were the case, deficit reduction would, indeed, increase our future standard of living (assuming that it didn't push us into a recession). It would do so by channeling output from consumption to private investment, as well as by reducing our foreign debt and future taxes.

On the other hand, *when deficit reduction results in a decrease in public investment* (as happened when President Clinton's investment programs were cut), *the impact on our future standard of living is unclear. In this case, private investment and foreign debt reduction are replacing public investment. The outcome depends on which of these alternative uses of our resources will be most beneficial for our children.*

One reason the deficit hawks have gained strength in recent years is the widespread perception that the huge Reagan deficits of the 1980s were spent on consumption (e.g., defense, Medicare, Medicaid, Social Security, and interest on the public debt). These deficits brought about high *real* interest rates (i.e., adjusted for inflation), which discouraged private investment[20] and increased foreign indebtedness.[21] In addition, public investment in training, infrastructure, and nondefense research and development was cut back during the Reagan era.[22]

Even though Ronald Reagan's fiscal policy contributed to the longest peacetime boom in our history, most economists agree with Benjamin Friedman that America went on a consumption binge and "billed the tab to the future."[23] Professor Friedman's indignation at President Reagan's deficits assumed biblical proportions. He began the first chapter of his book, *Day of Reckoning*, with a quote from Proverbs, "A good man leaveth an inheritance to his children's children." More prosaically, he said:

just as the federal deficit grew to record size in the 1980s, the share of federal spending devoted to potentially productivity-enhancing investment dwindled to an all-time low.[24]

Friedman's view is shared by many sophisticated analysts. Listen to Peter Peterson, a former secretary of commerce and economic adviser to President Nixon:

During the 1980s, a single president could congratulate himself on having sold twice as much federal debt to the public as all the cumulative paper issued by Presidents George Washington through Jimmy Carter. . . . By themselves debts and deficits are neither good nor bad. They are means to an end, which may or may not be constructive. Alas, our public debt is largely used to finance extra consumption, not extra investment. Indeed, even as the federal deficit has been rising, public investment has been declining.[25]

Not everyone, however, agrees with this perception of Reagan's deficits. The distinction between investment and consumption is sometimes fuzzy. For example, defense spending is usually categorized as consumption. But consider the argument of University of Michigan economist Edward Gramlich:

the 1980s boom in defense spending could have represented a form of investment. This boom may have put a strain on the Communist bloc, led to the breakdown of these economies and the collapse of the Warsaw Pact, made possible lower future levels of defense spending and taxes, and released resources for higher levels of future consumption. . . . It is obviously difficult to make judgments on this matter, but it is at least now not so clear that the defense-spending induced deficits of the 1980s were bad for the future living standards.[26]

Friedman, Peterson, and Gramlich all make valid arguments. The Reagan administration did cut nonmilitary public investment and crowd out private investment while boosting military spending. But since some of the military spending was designed to bring down the Soviet Union (and perhaps did), it seems questionable to label it all consumption. In addition, some of Reagan's military spending (such as defense-sponsored research and development[27]) appears to have enhanced worker productivity. Thus, it is hard to judge exactly how much Reagan affected overall investment.

3. PUBLIC INVESTMENT HAWKS

Economists agree that if certain types of investment projects are to be carried out, government support is essential; that is, some investments must be public. The reason? The private sector doesn't find these investments profitable. Put differently, under certain conditions the free market breaks down because it won't provide what people want. If the government doesn't boost the output of these products, they won't be adequately supplied. The government can stimulate production either by supplying the output itself or by motivating the private sector with purchases, tax breaks, or other incentives.

Some goods that the private sector won't adequately supply are national defense, public health, police and fire protection, justice administration, weather service, research, clean air and water, education, worker training, and infrastructure. What these goods have in common is that a large portion of their benefits are *external*.[28] An external benefit is one from which you can't be excluded. You can't be charged a price for an *external benefit* because you freely enjoy it anyway. External benefits pour down on you like the rain. Think about clean air, for example. Can you imagine charging people a fee for breathing clean air? It wouldn't work. They'd breathe it anyway. Since there is no way to charge a price for such goods, the private sector has no incentive to supply them, even though people may place a high value on them. *To the extent that a good generates external benefits, the free market will fail to supply it. The government must step in.*

By contrast, an *internal benefit* is one from which you *can* be excluded. If you don't pay the price for that hamburger or that shirt, you don't enjoy them. Since you can be made to pay for such goods, supplying them can be profitable for private firms. *To the extent that a good possesses internal benefits, the free market can adequately supply it.*

Goods can differ enormously in the proportion of their benefits that are internal versus external. Clean air or police protection, for example, provides benefits that are overwhelmingly external. Such goods are called *public goods*.[29] On the other hand, such products as hamburgers and shirts possess mostly internal benefits. Goods like these are referred to as *private goods*.

Many goods are mixtures, providing significant external as well as internal benefits. The private sector will supply less of these goods than people want, producing them only to the extent that their benefits are internal. Economists recommend subsidies and other government incentives to bolster the output of such goods.

Consider education. There are benefits that you alone derive from your education, such as increased skills leading to higher income. But there are also external benefits, that is, benefits that spill over onto others. For example, your education increases your productivity, adding to society's income and taxes. It also makes you a more informed citizen, more capable of knowledgeable participation in the democratic process. Consequently, if education were left to the private sector, too little would be provided. The need for government support is universally recognized.

Research and development are another example of a public/private good. An industry that undertakes research and development generates benefits for itself. It also generates external benefits, benefits for people who do not buy that industry's products. For example, other firms build on this industry's inventions. Thus, the benefits the industry creates exceed the benefits it can profit from. Put differently, the industry loses profits because it can't prevent other firms from snatching some of the gains it has produced. To the extent that the profits of research and development can't be completely appropriated by the industry that undertakes them, too few resources flow into this activity unless it is subsidized by the government. For this reason, governments should and do support research and development.

A classic example of the inability of a firm to capture the full monetary value of an invention is the development of the transistor by Bell Labs.[30] The benefits of the transistor spilled over onto firms all over the globe: the television industry in Japan, the automobile industry in Germany, and the computer industry in the United States. Meanwhile, the royalties accruing to Bell Labs were very small. Case studies have demonstrated that the value to society of inventions averages about three times the value to the inventor.[31]

As Peter Peterson put it, in recommending a tax credit for research and development:

From the invention of the transistor and the superconductor to the development of genetic cloning and fiber optics, great commercial discoveries have generated benefits for the entire economy that far surpass the profits of the discoverer. Most economists have always known this, and many have long advocated preferential incentives for the sort of research and development likely to lead to "public benefit" discoveries.[32]

Worker training is another example of a public/private good. Firms derive internal benefits from worker training, since more productive workers generate more profits. But some of the benefits are external. Workers can leave the firm that has trained them, bestowing the benefits of their enhanced productivity on other firms. Since no firm can appropriate all the benefits of its worker-training program, firms will underinvest in their workers. This reasoning supports public investment in worker training.[33]

Economists not only agree that some investments must be public but also acknowledge that in some cases public investment is more beneficial for our future standard of living than private investment.

Even a passionate deficit hawk like Benjamin Friedman supports this view:

some forms of public investment may enhance productivity just as much as, and perhaps even more than, private investment.[34]

There is considerable evidence that education, worker training, and research and development are public investments that would greatly enhance future productivity.[35] Another promising area for public investment is the improvement of transportation and communication. As Alice Rivlin observes:

The deterioration and congestion of highways and airports is visible and annoying to many Americans and extremely costly in terms of lost time and repair bills . . . few doubt that improving infrastructure would boost productivity.[36]

Rivlin also points out that we have neglected hazards from nuclear waste. Cleaning up this damage is not a profitable venture for the private sector. It would require an enormous *public* investment, an investment that would provide incalculable benefits for future generations.

In a 1991 study, the CBO examined the effects on productivity of public investment in such areas as infrastructure, worker training, and research and development. The CBO concluded:

this study finds that spending in each of the public capital areas considered may yield returns greater than the average rate of return to private investment. Such high returns, however, can be expected only on carefully selected spending projects.[37]

Not only did President Clinton lose investment projects to spending caps left over from the budget agreement of 1990, but he sacrificed even more in his five-year deficit-reduction agreement of 1993. Columnists who had been influential deficit hawks criticized Clinton for submitting to the deficit-cutting pressures they themselves helped to create. Many public investments endorsed by these pundits were cut back, such as worker training, education, mass transit, and technological research.[38] According to President Clinton's labor secretary, Robert Reich, less than 40% of Clinton's education and training initiatives were saved. But, as both Bob Woodward and Elizabeth Drew have documented, the political pressures to balance the budget were overwhelming, and the deficit phobia still gripping the nation promises further cuts in the future.

It is ironic that deficit hawks have helped bring about reductions in many public investments that they supported. In claiming that deficits impoverish our children, they ignored the fact that government borrowing *can* promote the well-being of our children. Cutting deficits for the sake of cutting deficits is a meat-ax approach, leading to the elimination of projects that could be vital for future generations. I wonder if these deficit hawks are horrified at what they have wrought.

4. PUBLIC INVESTMENT AND THE DEFICIT

Politicians and pundits frequently assert that state and local governments are not allowed to incur deficits. It isn't true. These governments borrow all the time, issuing bonds for such investment projects as roads, schools, parks, and water systems. They just don't label the borrowing "deficit spending." They call it *capital expenditure* and record it on a separate budget called a *capital budget*. Sounds a lot less scary than deficit spending, doesn't it?

The budget used by state and local governments for operating or current outlays is called the *operating or current budget*. It is the current budget that state and local governments are legally required to balance. The capital budget is expected to run a "deficit."

Is this dual budget system unusual? Not at all. It follows standard principles of accounting. It is practiced not only by state and local governments but by private businesses. If there were no separate capital accounts, corporations would continuously be reporting deficits or losses. Every industrial country I am aware of, except the United States, provides separate measures of current and capital expenditures.

Here is what Baumol and Blinder say about deficit spending on investment projects:

Some federal spending goes to purchase capital of various sorts—government buildings, military equipment, and so on. There is nothing unusual about borrowing to purchase assets. Private businesses and individuals do it all the time. For this reason, many people have suggested that the federal government compile a separate capital budget, just as most state and local governments now do.[39]

I believe our federal government should adopt a dual accounting system in which borrowing is recorded on a separate budget, a capital budget. Why? Because of the widely accepted value judgment that those who benefit should pay the cost. Under such a system, consumption (current) expenditures would be recorded on the current budget and would normally be financed by taxes.[40] Public investment expenditures, which generate their benefits in the future, would be recorded on the capital budget and would be financed by borrowing. The interest costs of the borrowing would be borne in the future. If you accept the value judgment that those who benefit should pay, you will probably agree that we should finance entitlements and other consumption expenditures out of taxes and finance investment by borrowing.[41]

Are dual budgets just a gimmick? I don't think so. This accounting procedure shows us how we are paying for various expenditures, whether by taxing or by borrowing. Currently, it is impossible to know. *The capital budget links an investment project with the requisite borrowing.* Legislators and voters would have to be persuaded that each investment project was worth borrowing for. *The current budget links government outlays for consumption with the requisite taxes.* Legislators and voters would have to be convinced that each *current* expenditure was worth being taxed for.

As a general rule, the current budget should be balanced. This rule would need to be relaxed, however, if the country slipped into a recession. An economic slump, remember, results in an automatic deficit. The automatic deficit, due to falling tax revenues and rising public assistance, will show up in the current budget. It reflects the operation of the automatic stabilizer, which cushions the fall in employment.[42] *In a recession the current budget should run a deficit.* Conversely, if the economy becomes overheated, the current budget should register a surplus.

If a fiscal stimulus were needed to counteract a recession, a structural deficit could be incurred as well. This deficit could appear in either budget. If the government elected to increase employment by boosting consumption spending, the deficit would appear in the current budget, resulting from an increase in entitlements and/or a reduction in income taxes. If the government decided to increase employment by expanding investment, the deficit would appear in the capital budget. (The reverse also holds. If a fiscal contraction were needed in order to fight inflation, the government could run a surplus in the current budget and/or postpone investments in the capital budget.)

As an example of how dual budgeting helps people perceive the link between financing and spending, consider my state of North Carolina. Soundings of voters in 1993 revealed they were angry about current taxes and didn't want to pay another cent. To everyone's surprise, these same voters approved a bond issue of $740 million earmarked for parks, water projects, community colleges, and the state university system. Interviews quoted in the local paper showed that the voters felt this borrowing would generate enough benefits in the future to justify the cost. "We need to improve the schools, the water systems, and the parks. It's important for the children," said Diane Johnston of Durham. "I think it's good for the children. We need to educate our children," said Ivy Farrow.[43]

Bob Scott, ex-governor of North Carolina and president of the state's community college system, reacted to the voter approval by saying:

The community support has been very gratifying. People recognize that community colleges do improve people's skills. They recognize that we are talking about jobs and about income—for our people and for this state.[44]

Another benefit of a dual budget could be that the emotion-laden term "deficit" might fall out of use. *We don't refer to borrowing by entities that employ a capital budget as "deficit spending."*[45] We don't say that General Motors is incurring a deficit when it borrows to construct a new plant; or when the state of North Carolina borrows for highways or libraries; or when you borrow to put your children through college or to buy a house. Why not? Perhaps because a capital budget *links the borrowing and the spending*, thereby making it apparent that the other side of the debt is an asset. General Motors, North Carolina, and you have all incurred a debt, but on the other side of the ledger, you have also generated an asset. *If the debt is also creating an asset, where is the deficit?*[46]

As Robert Eisner put it:

Recognizing that the federal government, unlike private business and most state and local governments, has no separate capital budget, we should be especially resistant to deficit reducers who would destroy the nation's wealth. . . .

The public has feared that budget deficits add to their own debt burden and that of future generations. What we really bequeath to the future, however, is our physical and human capital. A "deficit" which finances construction and maintenance of our roads, bridges, harbors, and airports is an investment in the future. So are expenditures to preserve and enhance our natural resources, or to educate our people and keep them healthy.[47]

Robert Heilbroner and Peter Bernstein made a rough estimate of the investments that would have been recorded on a capital budget in 1988.[48] They found that public investment totaled about $100 billion—$55 billion in states and municipalities and $40 by the federal government. In that high-employment year the official deficit incurred by all levels of government was $98.3 billion.[49] Had we used a dual budget, we would have recorded that the current budget was approximately balanced in 1988, while the capital budget registered borrowing of $100 billion for investment in the future.

If we accept Heilbroner and Bernstein's estimates, does that mean we endorse the federal government's fiscal behavior in 1988? Not at all. We might disagree with who was taxed and how the government spent its money. But there is one accusation we could not make: we could not accuse the government of borrowing for consumption and sticking future generations with the cost.

5. PUBLIC INVESTMENT: PORK OR PROGRESS?

Why hasn't our federal government adopted a dual budget? According to Robert Heilbroner, the answer lies in the deep distrust, even cynicism, that Americans have come to feel for government-supported projects:

This distrust was not always there. The government financed the transcontinental railway system, the Panama Canal, the TVA dams and the interstate highway system, all with strong public support. Only during the last decade has belief in the constructive economic use of government largely disappeared.[50]

The benefits from investment projects like these are heavily *external*.[51] Consequently, the private sector will fail to adequately provide them. Without government help, they will be undersupplied.

Economists agree that when external benefits are substantial, government support is needed. By training, however, economists are skeptical about the ability of government decision makers to improve on the market. Economic policy is, after all, a political process. Too often subsidies benefit specific politicians rather than the nation as a whole. Government funds are channeled into pork instead of productive projects. Egregious porcine specimens are easy to find: in 1991 Congress laid out $500,000 for a museum honoring Lawrence Welk in his birthplace, Strasburg, North Dakota. In 1993, Congress spent $58 million to bail out the shipbuilding company of George Steinbrenner, owner of the New York Yankees.[52]

Listen to Charles L. Schultze, chief economic adviser to President Jimmy Carter:

the federal government has sporadically supported several large-scale projects aimed at commercially feasible new technologies: the Clinch River breeder reactor, the supersonic transport (SST), and several large projects undertaken to learn how to gasify coal and extract oil from shale are among the most prominent. . . . Most often these federal government ventures into commercial R&D [research and development] projects have yielded highly disappointing results. Few became commercial successes, but, as might be expected, most were kept going even after it became obvious they would not be successful.[53]

Despite disappointing results in individual cases, the large external benefits resulting from research and development led Schultze to the widely held view that government support for these projects should be increased. As Robert Heilbroner and Lester Thurow argued:

The key to the American future lies in changing our mind about the role of government in the economy . . . this means undertaking a long-overdue investment program in infrastructure, including education.[54]

While endorsing an increase in public investment, Schultze, Heilbroner, Thurow, and many other economists also recommend institutional changes designed to avoid pork. They say *administrative mechanisms need to be created that take the politics out of the allocation of funds between competing investment projects*. A model might be the peer review process used by the National Institutes of Health, where experts not beholden to politicians determine which research projects merit support. Another apparently successful arrangement has been the blue-ribbon commission set up to select the military bases to be closed due to cutbacks in military spending.[55] A further possibility would be to select some respected and nonpartisan body (such as the CBO) to determine which expenditures can be classified as investment.

Without new procedures and institutions to insulate government subsidies from politics, pork could be as likely an outcome of government spending as progress.[56] Pork is one reason some economists are dubious about adopting a dual budget, even though they may favor it in principle. These economists feel such a budget would open a Pandora's box of political infighting over what is and what is not "investment." If Senator X gets his pork defined as "investment" and included in the capital budget, Senator Y will try to do the same.

6. THE IMPACT OF DEFICIT PHOBIA

I fear that deficit phobia will make our economy recession-prone.[57] Cutting deficits reduces spending. We rely on the Fed to lower interest rates in order to counteract this decline. But the Fed may not be able to lower interest rates enough to maintain total spending against a stampede to eliminate the deficit. I'm not the only economist to worry about this future possibility. Here is the warning of the CBO:

Most economists would say that doing the job quickly . . . could severely disrupt the economy.[58]

As the economic advisers to the Clinton administration put it:

the central objective of deficit reduction was and remains *expenditure switching*—away from consumption and . . . toward investment. The lower interest rates brought about by deficit reduction are the way the market accomplishes this expenditure switching. . . . some people worry that deficit reduction might retard [income] growth in the short run by siphoning off aggregate demand. Such a concern is justified. Deficit reduction *by itself* certainly does tend to contract the economy. After all, raising taxes and cutting government spending reduce the demand for goods and services.[59]

If deficit reduction does decrease total spending, private investment is unlikely to be stimulated. In fact, research shows that when total spending decreases, private investment also tends to decline, even though interest rates are lower.[60] A drop in total spending lowers sales and output. Why should businesses invest (that is, add to their capacity) when their output is falling short of their existing capacity?

Even if deficit reduction works as the deficit hawks hope—switching consumption into private investment without precipitating a depression—it may not be the best way to benefit our children. Increasing *public* investment might produce greater future benefits. *Instead of reducing government borrowing, we could switch the borrowed funds from consumption to public investment.* Future generations might be better served by *public* investment in such areas as education, research, health, information systems, airports, highways, bridges, mass transit, public housing and toxic waste cleanup than by *private* investment in factories, equipment, machinery, housing, autos, televisions, VCRs, and appliances.

Every dollar we extract from consumption is freed for private investment plus a decrease in our foreign debt, for public investment, or for any combination of the two. If consumption is reduced through deficit reduction, the resulting decrease in interest rates stimulates private investment and reduces foreign debt[61] (assuming no recession). On the other hand, if deficit spending is switched from consumption to public investment, our budget deficit and our indebtedness to foreigners are not directly affected.

How do we choose?

A key question is this: *Which type of investment will have a larger positive impact on our future well-being?* If public investment boosts our future standard of living sufficiently, then the larger debt costs resulting from this public investment could be more than offset by a corresponding benefit. (Keep in mind that our standard of living includes benefits that may not show up in our national income statistics but that affect our quality of life, such as reduced crime, a cleaner environment, better recreation facilities, reduced traffic congestion, and safer airlines.) Also, if the deficit-financed public investment causes our national income to grow faster than deficit reduction would, the debt–GDP ratio could eventually be lower with public than with private investment. Moreover, even if the debt–GDP ratio were higher under public investment, you might feel the additional interest charges were worth the additional benefits.

Suppose you prefer that *some* of the decreased consumption be channeled into public investment. In return for sacrificed consumption, you may, for example, favor an increase in spending on mass transit or toxic waste cleanup. *Deficit aversion will work against you.* You may find—as President Clinton has—that the projects you value are being slashed in order to reduce or avoid a deficit.

Many economists believe that avoiding deficits will cause the elimination of public investments that are crucial to the quality of life we pass on to our children. On December 1, 1994, over 400 economists including eight Nobel laureates issued a statement urging an increase in public investment. The statement said, in part:

There is a danger in the current anti-government tone of our national political discourse that we as a nation will forget the essential economic contribution made by public investment in our people and in our infrastructure.

Just as business must continually reinvest in order to prosper, so must a nation. Higher productivity—the key to higher living standards—is a function of public, as well as private investment.

If America is to succeed in an increasingly competitive world, we must expand efforts to equip our children with better education and our workers with more advanced skills. We must assure that disadvantaged children arrive at school age healthy and alert. We must prevent drug abuse and dropping out among teenagers. We must fix our bridges and expand our airports. We must rebuild our inner cities. We must accelerate the diffusion of technology to small- and medium-sized businesses.[62]

Can't these public investment projects simply be taken over by state and local governments as so many politicians are currently recommending? Most economists say no. These governments typically underspend on investment because so many of the benefits spill over onto other states and localities. Federal support is needed.

NOTES

1. Recognizing the shortcomings of the GDP as a measure of economic well-being, economists have begun to develop a more accurate measure called net economic welfare (NEW). This measure includes such items as the value of leisure, the services of homemakers, do-it-yourself work, and underground activity. Deducted are such items as environmental damage.

2. *The Age of Diminished Expectations* by Paul Krugman, pp. 7–8.

3. *Reviving the American Dream* by Alice Rivlin, pp. 65–66.

4. Ibid., p. 45. An additional factor was the migration of workers from farming to manufacturing, where the productivity was higher.

5. The causes of our productivity slowdown are not yet clear. See, for example, *Peddling Prosperity* by Paul Krugman, ch. 4, or *Growth with Equity* by Martin N. Baily, Gary Burtless, and Robert E. Litan, ch. 2.

6. *Reviving the American Dream* by Alice Rivlin, p. 68.

7. Discretionary spending is limited by yearly congressional appropriations. By contrast, entitlements are determined by statutory formulas and eligibility requirements and are not subject to any dollar ceiling.

8. According to the CBO, these spending caps are being successfully enforced. They were renewed for another five years in the budget agreement of 1993. See *Reducing the Deficit: Spending and Revenue Options*, Congress of the United States, Congressional Budget Office, March 1994, p. 6.

9. *The Agenda* by Bob Woodward, pp. 156, 161–62.

10. Ibid., p. 163.

11. *On the Edge: The Clinton Presidency* by Elizabeth Drew, p. 166.

12. *The Agenda* by Bob Woodward, p. 166.

13. Ibid., p. 155.

14. Symmetrically, U.S. residents find foreign securities less attractive, which helps increase the value of the dollar relative to foreign currencies.

15. *Day of Reckoning* by Benjamin Friedman, pp. xiii, 9–11.

16. *The Debt and the Deficit* by Robert Heilbroner and Peter Bernstein, p. 116.

17. *Reviving the American Dream* by Alice Rivlin, pp. 6–7.

18. *The Washington Post National Weekly Edition*, September 26–October 2, 1994, p. 10.

19. To be more accurate, "government spending on consumption" should sometimes read "government transfers inducing mostly consumption spending," since cutting Social Security, for example, is only a reduction in a transfer payment, which causes the recipient to reduce mostly consumption spending. Medicare, on the other hand, is largely consumption spending by the government.

20. Lawrence Summers has estimated that for every dollar increase in the

federal deficit, private net investment falls by about 40¢, and foreign indebtedness increases by about 25¢. For a discussion of this study, see *Reagan and the Economy* by Michael J. Boskin (San Francisco, Calif.: ICS Press, 1987), pp. 191–192. A study by the CBO produced similar results. See *The Economic and Budget Outlook: Fiscal Years 1994–1998*, Congress of the United States, Congressional Budget Office, January 1993, p. 76. Some economists argue that the high interest rates of the 1980s crowded out net exports but had little effect on private investment. For this argument, see Alan Blinder's article "Is the National Debt Really—I Mean Really—a Burden" in *Debt and the Twin Deficits Debate*, edited by James M. Rock, pp. 212–213.

21. A study by Benjamin Friedman reveals that real interest rates on commercial paper in the 1980s averaged about 5%, as compared with −.11% (yes, that's a minus) in the 1970s, 1.74% in the 1960s, and .8% in the 1950s. Friedman also reported that gross investment in machinery and plant trended down throughout the 1980s and reached 9.8% in 1989. In addition, the trade deficit of $25 billion in 1980 climbed to $160 billion by 1987. See "U.S. Fiscal Policy in the 1980s: Consequences of Large Budget Deficits at Full Employment," by Benjamin Friedman in *Debt and the Twin Deficits Debate*, edited by James M. Rock. (See p. 153 for the real interest rates, pp. 151–152 for investment, and p. 157 for the trade deficit.)

22. For details on the cuts in public, nonmilitary investment under the Reagan administration, see "The Supply-Side Consequences of U.S. Fiscal Policy in the 1980s" by M. A. Akhtar and Ethan S. Harris in *Federal Reserve Bank of New York Quarterly Review* (Spring 1992), pp. 1–20. Public nonmilitary investment (at all levels of government) dropped to 1% of GDP compared to 3% of GDP in the 1950s and 1960s. See *Peddling Prosperity* by Paul Krugman, p. 127.

23. *Day of Reckoning* by Benjamin Friedman, p. 4.

24. Ibid., p. xvi.

25. *Facing Up* by Peter Peterson, p. 63.

26. *Debt and the Twin Deficits Debate*, edited by James M. Rock, pp. 178–179. For support of Gramlich's argument, see *The Rise of Russia and the Fall of the Soviet Union* by John B. Dunlop, p. 4. Dunlop points out that Soviet economic growth had virtually come to a halt during the years 1978–1985 and that this had been compounded by the arms buildup of the Reagan government. For a supporting view, see *Debt and Taxes* by John Makin and Norman Ornstein, p. 272.

27. See "The Supply-Side Consequences of U.S. Fiscal Policy in the 1980s" by M. A. Akhtar and Ethan S. Harris in *Federal Reserve Bank of New York Quarterly Review* (Spring 1992), p. 9. Akhtar and Harris argue that the increase in defense research and development under Reagan "probably offset some of the adverse effect of lower non-defense R&D." They point out that "defense

R&D activities have been managed with a view to exploiting commercial opportunities. For example, major advances in civil aviation, medical technology
and weather satellites originated from defense-sponsored R&D.''

28. See, for example, *Economics*, 7th ed., by William Baumol and Alan
Blinder, pp. 304–313.

29. There is another characteristic that defines a public good: additional consumers do not deplete the supply and can therefore benefit with negligible cost
to society. Consider a bridge. Once the bridge is built, additional users add little
or no cost. If a private firm were allowed to build the bridge and charge people
for using it, people who could not pay would be excluded, even though letting
them use the bridge would incur a negligible cost. Under such circumstances,
it makes sense for the government to supply the good or subsidize it. See, for
example, ibid., 7th ed., p. 310.

30. See *Economics*, 14th ed., by Paul Samuelson and William Nordhaus, p.
311.

31. Ibid., p. 188.

32. *Facing Up* by Peter Peterson, p. 297.

33. Ibid., p. 298. Another rationale for worker training is that it tends to
reduce the gap between the rich and the poor. I discuss this issue in the next
chapter.

34. *Day of Reckoning* by Benjamin Friedman, p. xv.

35. For an excellent study on this issue, see *How Federal Spending for Infrastructure and Other Public Investments Affects the Economy*, Congress of the
United States, Congressional Budget Office, July 1991. This study shows especially high rates of return from federally funded research and development in
science, engineering, health, and agriculture; from public investment in airport
capacity, highway maintenance projects, and water resources; and from federal
spending on education and training, such as Job Corps. See also *Reviving the
American Dream* by Alice Rivlin, ch. 4.

36. *Reviving the American Dream* by Alice Rivlin, p. 69.

37. *How Federal Spending for Infrastructure and Other Public Investments
Affects the Economy*, July 1991, Congress of the United States, Congressional
Budget Office, p. 3. For other evidence that public investments are highly productive, see *Growth with Equity* by M. N. Baily, G. Burtless, and R. E. Litan,
ch. 6.

38. See, for example, the *New York Times* editorial of July 26, 1993, and
David Broder in the *Washington Post Weekly*, August 16–22, 1993, p. 4.

39. *Economics*, 7th ed., by William Baumol and Alan Blinder, p. 755.

40. This value judgment is reflected in the budget agreements of 1990 and
1993, which require that increases in entitlements be tax financed. See *Reducing
the Deficit: Spending and Revenue Options*, Congress of the United States, Congressional Budget Office, March 1994, pp. 4–6.

41. Not all entitlements are necessarily consumption. Some might be cate-

gorized as "investments" to the extent that they enhance the future productivity of the workforce, such as child health care or antipoverty programs.

42. See Chapter 2, Section 6.

43. *The Raleigh News and Observer*, November 3, 1993, p. 10A.

44. Ibid.

45. See Robert Heilbroner in *The New York Review of Books*, November 19, 1992, p. 12.

46. A similar point would hold for a deficit emerging during a recession; the offsetting benefit would be the jobs created.

47. *How Real Is the Deficit?* by Robert Eisner, p. 179.

48. *The Debt and the Deficit* by Robert Heilbroner and Peter Bernstein, pp. 81–85, 117–120. See similar calculations for the federal government by Benjamin Zycher in *Jobs and Capital*, published by the Milken Institute for Job and Capital Formation, Summer 1992, p. 10. Zycher combines federal expenditures for physical capital and R&D for defense and nondefense along with outlays on nondefense education and training from 1980 through 1992. He finds that the current federal budget ran tiny surpluses (between $34 and $50 billion) in the full-employment years of 1987, 1988, and 1989. The official federal budget deficits for these years was $175.3 billion for both 1987 and 1988 and $166 billion for 1989.

49. *Economic Report of the President*, 1992, Table B-78.

50. Robert Heilbroner in *The New York Review of Books*, November 19, 1992, p. 12.

51. See Section 3 in this chapter.

52. *USA Today*, January 19, 1995, p. 6A.

53. *Memos to the President* by Charles L. Schultze, pp. 302–306.

54. *Economics Explained* by Robert Heilbroner and Lester Thurow, pp. 258–259.

55. See the article by Eric Schmitt in the *New York Times* on January 27, 1995.

56. See the case studies of federal support of research and development in *The Technology Pork Barrel* by Linda R. Cohen and Roger G. Noll.

57. See Chapter 2, Section 9.

58. See *The Economic and Budget Outlook: Fiscal Years 1994–1998*, Congress of the United States, Congressional Budget Office, January, 1993, p. 71.

59. *Economic Report of the President*, 1994, p. 36.

60. *The Misunderstood Economy* by Robert Eisner, p. 39.

61. See Section 2 of this chapter.

62. Statement issued on January 19, 1995, by The Economic Policy Institute, 1730 Rhode Island Avenue NW, Washington, DC 20036.

4

The Rich, the Poor,
and the Deficit

Jobs and growth are still not everything. *Fairness* is an additional dimension of economic well-being. How is our national income distributed? Does it go to just a favored few, or is it widely distributed?

1. OUR GROWING INCOME INEQUALITY

From 1947 to 1973, our rapidly increasing prosperity was shared by all income levels. This has not been so for more than 20 years. Since 1973, especially during the 1980s, the inequality in our incomes increased dramatically.[1] The rich got richer, the poor got poorer, and middle-income families barely held their own. From 1980 to 1990, the average after-tax income of the bottom 10% of the population fell from $4,785 to $4,295 (adjusting for inflation). Those in the middle saw a minuscule increase in their average take-home pay during this decade. At the same time the average after-tax income of the top 10% rose from $75,568 to $106,638. For the top 1%, the increase was from $213,416 to $399,697.[2]

During the Reagan years, our huge deficits benefited the rich and hurt the poor.[3] Tax rates on the wealthy were cut. The theory was that the extra income made available through these tax cuts would ''trickle down'' and benefit people at all income levels. It didn't happen. To make matters worse, the tax burden on the poor increased, due to rising payroll and state sales taxes.[4] During the years from 1980 to 1985, taxes on the average family in the bottom 20% of the income scale increased by $137, while taxes on the average family in the top 20% *decreased* by $2,513.[5]

Under Reagan, changes in transfer payments also favored the rich. Social Security payments to the affluent increased, while assistance to the poor declined, due to cuts in such programs as Aid to Families with Dependent Children (AFDC), food stamps, and public housing.[6] From 1979 to 1989, cash transfers to the poorest 20% of families fell by 13%, while transfers to the richest 20% increased by 20%.[7]

As Paul Krugman has described it:

If one bears in mind that tax rates for the well-off generally fell in the Reagan years, while noncash benefits for the poor, like public housing, became increasingly scarce, one sees a picture of simultaneous growth in wealth and poverty unprecedented in the twentieth century.[8]

2. DEFICIT HAWKS AND THE RICH VERSUS THE POOR

How does deficit reduction affect the gap between the rich and the poor? That depends on how it is achieved. Some deficit hawks want to balance the budget on the backs of the poor, and some on the backs of the rich. In the debate over the budget agreement of 1993, a major conflict erupted over whether to reduce the deficit by increasing taxes on the wealthy or by cutting assistance to the poor. Without Republican support, President Clinton and the Democrats incorporated into the five-year deficit-reduction plan an increase in the tax rate on the wealthy and a tax credit for income earned by the working poor.

In the wake of the Republican landslide of November 1994, the debate heated up again. Contrast the welfare proposals of President Clinton with those of the Republican Speaker of the House, Newt Gingrich. Gingrich proposed cutting around $45 billion over five years from food, housing, and income programs that assist the poor, including the disabled and the needy elderly. Gingrich sees welfare spending as a trap, enticing the poor into dependent and self-destructive behavior. He asserts that such programs promote a ''counterculture value system'' and ''ruin the poor.''[9] President Clinton sees them as a safety net that protects needy people from destitution and wants to preserve them.

A third approach has been proposed by the Concord Coalition, formed in 1992. These deficit hawks urge the curbing of entitlements, such as

Social Security and Medicare, arguing that they include handouts to the well-off. Foremost among this group were Senator Paul Tsongas, Democratic candidate for president in 1992, and Republican Senator Warren Rudman, who, together with economist Peter Peterson, founded the coalition. Ross Perot, an independent candidate for president in 1992, is also a supporter.

The main goal of the Concord Coalition was to reverse our consumption binge in order to increase investment. The best way to do this, they argued, was to bring down the deficit by cutting entitlements to the affluent. Reducing these entitlements decreases consumption. The money saved can then be channeled into investment. The position of the Concord Coalition is laid out in Peter Peterson's book *Facing Up*.

As Senators Tsongas and Rudman put it in the foreword to Peterson's book:

To cut the deficit we must . . . enact concrete reforms in our trillion-dollar system of federal entitlements from Social Security, Medicare, and civil service and military pensions to farm supports and to the employer-paid health-care exclusion. We must direct our reform efforts to where these programs provide windfalls to those who don't really need them. . . .

[This is] a blueprint for shifting from a consumption-based to . . . [an] investment-based economy.

Peterson is indignant that entitlements go to those who don't need them rather than to those who do:

Why does our single largest housing entitlement [the home mortgage interest deduction] give 80% of its benefits to households with incomes over $50,000— and nothing to households that cannot afford a home? . . . Why do we dole out special benefits to half a million successful peanut growers, dairy farmers, wheat growers, and honey producers—but leave over 3 million children to grow up in households reporting annual cash incomes of less that $5000? [10]

Taking into account both federal entitlement spending and tax loopholes, Peterson estimated that about half of all federal benefits go to households earning more than $30,000 a year and 25% to households earning more than $50,000.[11] He found that in 1991, the total federal benefits received by the average household earning under $10,000 was $5,700, while the total federal benefits received by the average household earning over $100,000 was $9,300. Peterson also calculated that Social

Security and Medicare recipients were getting back much more than they paid in.[12]

Cutting entitlements is easier said than done. The issue is politically explosive. No one wants to give up his or her share of the federal largesse. Consider the memo of Alice Rivlin, then President Clinton's budget director, that was leaked to the press shortly before the election of November 1994. The memo surveyed possible ways of bringing down the deficit, including cuts in Social Security and Medicare. Although the memo merely cataloged these possibilities without recommending any of them, it brought down a firestorm of accusations and denials. As the reporter Michael Kramer described it:

Poor Alice Rivlin. She told the truth and is getting burned for it. Democrats, including Bill Clinton, have disavowed her list of "illustrative options." Republicans, distorting her discussion of possible tax increases and entitlement cuts, are running television spots attacking her. Rivlin is simply doing her job.[13]

Deficit hawks focused on entitlements because they are projected to be the fastest growing component of federal spending for the foreseeable future.[14] The two big health care programs, Medicare and Medicaid, are expected to grow by 10% or more a year from 1994 to 2004, increasing from 3.7% to 6.3% of GDP. During this decade, other entitlements, including Social Security, are expected to consume a constant proportion of GDP. However, in the decades following 2010, as the baby boomers retire, there is expected to be a surge in Social Security benefits.

In order solve this problem, President Clinton appointed a 32-member, bipartisan panel called the Entitlement and Tax Reform Commission, headed by Senators Bob Kerrey (D-Nebr.) and John Danforth (R-Mo.). After spending ten months and more than $1.8 million, the commission threw up its hands. It had failed to come to any agreement about how to restrain the projected growth in Social Security and the other entitlement programs. All the commission could say was that "few easy and popular decisions are available to the American people" and that "tough action is needed sooner or later."[15]

Why do we need "tough action"? Unless our GDP grows more rapidly than is currently anticipated, entitlements or other government expenditures will have to be cut, or increases in our future tax rates will be required, or the deficit will skyrocket. This looming threat is a major reason both the deficit hawks and the public investment hawks are urging a switch from consumption to investment. They want us to boost our future income sufficiently so that our children will be able to sustain the rising Social Security, Medicare, and Medicaid bills without a crushing increase in their tax burden. I look more closely at these future trends in the following chapter.

3. DEFICIT REDUCTION, RECESSIONS, AND POVERTY

Cutting the deficit by any method reduces spending. Unless the Fed can offset this fiscal contraction by lowering interest rates, deficit reduction may lead to recession. If the deficit is cut too rapidly, the Fed will be unable to prevent a slump. Research by Robert Eisner shows that over the past 25 years deficit reduction has typically decreased total spending and destroyed jobs. Recessions usually increase poverty.[16] In addition, since the poor are usually hurt more than the rich, recessions increase the gap between the rich and poor.

Listen to Alan Blinder:

When recessions draft men and women into the ranks of the unemployed, the disadvantaged go first; the privileged go last. . . . Every study I know of points in the same direction: while most of us lose ground in a recession, the poor lose relatively more.[17]

Not only are the working poor hurt during recessions, but so are families with no breadwinners, such as the elderly and the disabled, since these nonworking poor rely heavily on public assistance. During hard times, middle- and upper-income Americans are less willing to tolerate welfare programs.[18]

One goal of President Clinton's five-year budget agreement of 1993 was to reverse the growing chasm between the rich and poor. Will Clinton's program be successful? I think the matter is in doubt. *Budget cuts enacted under the spur of deficit reduction not only are likely to slash benefits for the poor but could also create a chronically sluggish economy.* What the poor get today from an earned income tax credit, they may lose tomorrow as unemployment increases and public assistance is reduced.

4. HELPING THE POOR—AND THE NOT SO POOR

During the 1980s, taxes and transfers widened the gap between the rich and the poor. But the biggest increase in income inequality resulted from changes in income *before* taxes and transfers.[19] Wages and salaries became more unequal because the earnings of the skilled rose relative to those of the unskilled. Technological progress appears to have altered production methods in favor of skilled workers.[20] Thus, during the 1980s the gap between the earnings of college graduates and high school graduates increased, after having declined in earlier years. From 1979 to 1987, median earnings of high school-educated men aged 25–34 dropped by 11%, while median earnings of college-educated men increased by 8%.[21]

Many economists believe this trend could be reversed by appropriate government policy. They recommend public investment programs to educate the unskilled and those in need of retraining. Since expenditures like these would generate benefits in the future, government borrowing could be justified. Such an investment could decrease income inequality by boosting the productivity and incomes of the poor. Moreover, as the poor gain, so does the rest of society, since the poor pay more taxes and require less public assistance. As Alice Rivlin argues:

an aggressive effort to improve the skills, education, and work incentives of less-skilled and less-educated young people and adults could be a policy "twofer." Such an effort could spur productivity growth and narrow income disparities at the same time.[22]

Economists Martin Baily, Gary Burtless, and Robert Litan also endorse this type of public investment:

A sensible strategy to improve the U.S. income distribution must emphasize the job opportunities and earning capacities of comparatively unskilled workers. These workers have suffered the greatest harm from recent economic trends. Most of their income is derived from earnings. Improving their ability to earn good wages will not only raise their family incomes thus reducing inequality, it can also accelerate economic growth.[23]

Mindless pressure to avoid deficits can result in cuts in worthwhile investment projects like these, projects that could enhance the productivity of the poor and thereby increase the incomes of all of us.

NOTES

1. For an analysis of trends in income distribution, see *Growth with Equity* by Martin N. Baily, Gary Burtless, and Robert E. Litan, ch. 3. As they point

out, the slowdown in productivity growth and the increasing inequality in incomes began around the same time. If there is a connection between these trends, economists haven't yet figured out what it is. For an examination of intergenerational income distribution, see *Generational Accounting* by Lawrence Kotlikoff.

2. *Chain Reaction* by Thomas Edsall and Mary Edsall, p. 220. For those in the middle, the average income, adjusted for inflation, rose from $22,078 to $22,608.

3. *Reviving the American Dream* by Alice Rivlin, p. 71.

4. Even though most working poor were removed from the income tax rolls during the 1980s, their net tax burden increased. See ibid., p. 71.

5. *Chain Reaction* by Thomas Edsall and Mary Edsall, pp. 160–161.

6. *Growth with Equity* by Martin N. Baily, Gary Burtless, and Robert E. Litan, p. 70.

7. Ibid., p. 68.

8. *The Age of Diminished Expectations* by Paul Krugman, pp. 19–20.

9. *New York Times*, Sunday, November 13, 1994, p. 1.

10. *Facing Up* by Peter Peterson, p. 112.

11. Ibid., p. 104.

12. Ibid., p. 106.

13. *Time*, November 7, 1994.

14. *The Economic and Budget Outlook: Fiscal Years 1995–1999*, Congress of the United States, Congressional Budget Office, March 1994, p. 29.

15. From wire reports, December 15, 1994.

16. *Reviving the American Dream* by Alice Rivlin, p. 59.

17. *Hard Heads, Soft Hearts* by Alan Blinder, p. 36.

18. *Growth with Equity* by Martin N. Baily, Gary Burtless, and Robert E. Litan, pp. 49–50.

19. *Reviving the American Dream* by Alice Rivlin, pp. 71–72.

20. Technological progress need not always have this effect. It could alter production methods to the advantage of the unskilled by simplifying the production process. See *Growth with Equity* by Martin N. Baily, Gary Burtless, and Robert E. Litan, p. 60.

21. *Reviving the American Dream* by Alice Rivlin, pp. 71–72.

22. Ibid., p. 72.

23. *Growth with Equity* by Martin N. Baily, Gary Burtless, and Robert E. Litan, p. 73.

5

The Baby Boomers
and the Future Deficit

1. A PROJECTED NIGHTMARE

To many, the future deficit is more of a nightmare than recent deficits. The specter of a runaway deficit beginning in the second decade of the next century is not just a myth. Economists are worried too.

The crunch is expected to begin when the wave of baby boomers (those born between 1946 and 1964) starts to retire in 2010.[1] They will then draw benefits from Social Security and Medicare. In addition, because the population will be aging, the labor force will grow more slowly.[2] The proportion of elderly is expected to rise due to a decline in fertility (number of births per woman) along with an increase in life expectancy. The number of people over 65 is projected to double between 1990 and 2030, while the number of working-age people (20–64) is expected to increase by only 25%.[3] Consequently, it is anticipated that the ratio of workers to retired will decline after 2010.[4] In 1990 each retired person was backed by 5 workers. By 2030, it is forecast that only 2.8 workers will support each retiree.[5]

If these projections materialize, we will be faced with the painful future choice of reducing our senior citizens' health, pension, or welfare benefits or cutting other government spending or raising taxes or allowing the debt–GDP ratio to climb.

2. FUTURE DEFICIT AND TAX SCENARIOS

The budget projections based on these demographics are grim.[6] The CBO forecasts the following changes from 1995 to 2030, assuming no alteration in our current tax laws or entitlement levels[7]: as a percent of GDP, Social Security, Medicare, and Medicaid are projected to grow from 9% to 18%, and the interest on the public debt from 2% to 20%. In addition, it is estimated that the deficit–GDP ratio will increase over this period from 2% to 26%, and the public debt–GDP ratio from 50% to 229%.[8]

Researchers caution that long-range forecasts like these are uncertain, since they are sensitive to guestimates about such variables as births, deaths, marriages, immigration, tax revenues, productivity, interest rates, and entitlement spending.

For what they're worth, however, these projections imply an increased tax burden on future workers if the current level of public benefits is maintained. One approach to measuring this increased tax burden is to calculate the "lifetime net tax rate" for different generations, that is, the present value of lifetime taxes minus government benefits as a percentage of income from wages and salaries.[9] This measure indicates that future generations face a lifetime net tax rate of 84% compared with only 34% for current generations.[10] Another calculation shows that a 70-year-old male retiring in 1989 will receive a present value of lifetime benefits less taxes of $46,100, while a 20-year-old male will make a lifetime payment to the government of $198,300.[11]

How much would we have to raise taxes today in order to maintain the level of entitlements with no change in our debt–GDP ratio? The required adjustment would be an increase in our total taxes (federal, state, and local) from the current level of about 31% of GDP to about 34%.[12] Such a tax rate would still place the United States among the lightest taxed industrial countries in the world. See Table 2.[13]

Were we to permanently maintain our debt–GDP ratio at the 1995 level of 50.2%, the CBO calculates that our deficit would decline from 2.2% of GDP to about 1.6%, where it would remain.[14] Such a strategy would be similar to the one adopted by the 15 member nations of the European Union. They have pledged to maintain their debt and deficit to GDP ratios at no more than 60% and 3%, respectively. This goal was specified in the Maastricht Treaty of 1991, which was intended to create a monetary union with a single European currency by 1999. (I examine the rationale for these European fiscal norms in Chapter 7.)

Table 2
Tax Share of GDP in Selected Countries, 1994

Country	Percentage of GDP	Country	Percentage of GDP
United States	31.5	Denmark	60.0
Japan	32.3	Finland	53.1
Germany	46.5	Greece	35.4
France	48.9	Ireland	41.6
Italy	44.9	Netherlands	51.4
United Kingdom	36.4	Norway	55.3
Canada	42.2	Portugal	45.7
Australia	32.9	Spain	39.0
Austria	47.5	Sweden	58.4
Belgium	51.1		

Source: Organization for Economic Cooperation and Development.

The balanced-budget target recently adopted in the United States is much harsher than the Maastricht goal.[15] Unlike the United States, European countries acknowledge the necessity for government borrowing for public investment, which is the reason they permit a permanent deficit.

3. REMEDIES

Three of the most widely recommended remedies for our future budget crisis are:

3.1. Increase the Age of Retirement

In 1950, a third of the men over 70 were in the labor force, while today that percentage has dropped to only 16.[16] Given the growing number of skilled Americans who reach their 70s in good health, many argue that we should encourage longer working lives. Such a policy would boost future revenues and reduce entitlement spending.

Congress has already taken a step in this direction by raising the retirement age for full benefits from 65 to 67, to be phased in from 2000 to 2027. Peter Peterson, one of the founders of the Concord Coalition, recommends a larger step. His plan would increase the eligibility age for full Social Security benefits by three months per year from 1996 to 2014 and fix it at 70 from then on, while continuing to allow early retirement at reduced benefits.[17]

3.2. An Affluence Test for Retirees

The CBO calculates that about 40% of Social Security benefits go to households with incomes above the population median. An affluence test would involve reducing the benefits going to the richer retirees. One such plan, also formulated by Peter Peterson,[18] would cut benefits by 10% for each $10,000 of annual incomes above $40,000. In addition, 85% of Social Security benefits would be subject to the federal income tax.

3.3. Correct the Bias in the Consumer Price Index

Our public benefits are indexed to the Consumer Price Index (CPI); that is, if the CPI rises by, say, 3%, the benefits automatically rise by 3%. If the CPI accurately measured changes in the cost of living, such an adjustment would be reasonable. It is, however, widely acknowledged that the CPI overstates the changes in the cost of living.[19] Consequently, the *real* value of Social Security and other public benefits increases every year. As economists Paul Masson and Michael Mussa of the International Monetary Fund express it:

Several studies of the consumer price indexes . . . suggest that these indexes overestimate the annual inflation rate by about 1 percentage point (or somewhat more) because they fail to account adequately for quality improvements, the introduction of new goods, and other phenomena. Correction of this distortion, compounded over three decades, would imply about a one-third reduction in spending on indexed public pension schemes.[20]

Moreover, revising the CPI downward would boost taxes for most of us, since deductions, exemptions, and tax brackets are linked to the price index.

These recommendations are reasonable approaches to solving our expected budget crisis. They reduce current deficits or increase surpluses by cutting entitlements and raising taxes. Consequently, they reduce the growth rate in the public debt. In addition, they are tailored to squeeze consumption and not public investment. They could therefore boost future GDP.[21] (Recall that depressing consumption drives down interest rates and increases our future GDP by stimulating private investment and shrinking our foreign indebtedness.)[22]

NOTES

1. *The Economic and Budget Outlook: Fiscal Years 1997–2006*, May 1996, Congress of the United States, Congressional Budget Office, p. 69.

2. The labor force is projected by the Social Security Administration to decrease from an average growth rate of .9% annually from 1989 to 2010 to .2% from 2010 to 2050. From 1969 to 1989, the average annual rate of increase in the labor force was 1.9%. The projected trend is due to an aging population along with the expectation that the rate of increase in the labor force participation of women will level off in the future.

3. The 1996 *Economic Report of the President* also focuses on the "total dependency ratio," that is, the ratio of children plus the elderly to workers. Due to the decline in fertility, the proportion of children in the population is expected to drop from 29% in 1990 to 24% in 2030. Consequently, the total dependency ratio does not give as grim a picture as the elderly–worker ratio. The total dependency ratio was .70 in 1990. In 2030, it is projected to be .79, which is not as high as it was in the 1960s, when it exceeded .9. Nevertheless, the *Economic Report* points out that "children demand different resources from society than the elderly," so it is important to look at both ratios. The *Report* does not, however, publish budget forecasts employing the total dependency ratio.

4. See, for example, *Budget Deficits and Debt: Issues and Options*, a symposium sponsored by the Federal Reserve Bank of Kansas City, August 31–September 2, 1995.

5. *The Economic and Budget Outlook: Fiscal Years 1997–2006*, May 1996, Congress of the United States, Congressional Budget Office, p. 70.

6. Economic studies label our current fiscal policy as "unsustainable"; that is, we eventually will have to cut government spending or boost taxes or spur the labor force or productivity into growing faster; otherwise, the projected debt–GDP ratio will increase for the foreseeable future. See, for example, *The Economic and Budget Outlook: Fiscal Years 1997–2006*, May 1996, Congress of the United States, Congressional Budget Office, p. 87. One exception to this gloomy prediction is a recent study by the economic historian Richard Sutch. See his article "Is Social Spending Out of Control?" in *Challenge*, May–June 1996, pp. 9–15.

7. *The Economic and Budget Outlook: Fiscal Years 1997–2006*, May 1996, Congress of the United States, Congressional Budget Office, p. 80. These projections assume that discretionary spending grows with inflation after 2006 and that the budget deficits push up interest rates, thereby slowing economic growth.

8. According to a projection of Kumiharu Shigehara, the chief economist of the OECD (Organization for Economic Cooperation and Development), the debt–GDP ratio might rise to 120% by contrast with the CBO's forecast of 229%. See the *Budget Deficits and Debt: Issues and Options*, a symposium sponsored by the Federal Reserve Bank of Kansas City, August 31–September 2, 1995, p. 79.

9. The "present value" of a stream of future taxes or benefits or income is the present value of an asset that would generate this stream of returns at an appropriate interest rate. See "Generational Accounts: A Meaningful Alternative to Deficit Accounting" by Alan Auerbach, Jagadeesh Gokhale, and Lawrence Kotlikoff in *Tax Policy and the Economy*, ed. L. H. Summers and D. Bradford, pp. 55–110.

10. *The Economic and Budget Outlook: Fiscal Years 1997–2006*, May 1996, Congress of the United States, Congressional Budget Office, pp. 87–88.

11. *Budget Deficits and Debt: Issues and Options*, a symposium sponsored by the Federal Reserve Bank of Kansas City, August 31–September 2, 1995, p. 34. While generational accounting is controversial because of arbitrary assumptions about the future, the CBO concludes that its qualitative conclusions "hold under a wide range of alternative assumptions." See *The Economic and Budget Outlook: Fiscal Years 1997–2006*, May 1996, Congress of the United States, Congressional Budget Office, p. 88.

12. The reason that small changes in revenues or spending are linked to huge changes in debt projections is that borrowing increases interest costs, which then require more borrowing to pay the interest, leading to a vicious cycle of soaring interest charges on the debt. As the CBO puts it, "Because even a relatively small imbalance between revenues and outlays can be significantly amplified by escalating interest costs, the [debt] projections do not necessarily imply that resolving the nation's budgetary problems would require huge changes in spending or revenues." See *The Economic and Budget Outlook: Fiscal Years 1997–2006*, May 1996, p. 83.

13. *Economic Report of the President*, February 1996, p. 81, Table 3.2. The data in the *Report* differ slightly from those in the OECD table. The *Report* shows that the federal, state, and local tax share of GDP in the United States in 1994 was 30.7% (pp. 280, 372). The *Report* calculates that federal receipts would have to increase by 3% of GDP to keep the debt–GDP ratio from rising (p. 83). This calculation implies that federal, state, and local taxes would have to rise from 30.7% of GDP to 33.6%.

14. See *The Economic and Budget Outlook: Fiscal Years 1997–2006*, May 1996, *Congress of the United States, Congressional Budget Office*, p. 89. Under such a plan the interest on the public debt, currently 3.5% of GDP, would level off at 2.7%.

15. The CBO calculates that a balanced budget would bring the debt–GDP ratio to 6% in 2050. On this trend they comment, "A balanced budget would

. . . put the United States back on its historical path of declining debt as a share of GDP during peace and prosperity. However, a ratio of debt to income as low as 6 percent would be unusual in modern history; the debt ratio has not been so low since America's entry into World War 1.'' *The Economic and Budget Outlook: Fiscal Years 1997–2006*, May 1996, Congress of the United States, Congressional Budget Office, p. 88.

16. ''Will America Grow Up Before It Grows Old?'' by Peter Peterson in *The Atlantic Monthly*, May 1996, p. 73.

17. ''Solutions for Developed Economies'' by Peter Peterson in *Budget Deficits and Debt: Issues and Options*, a symposium sponsored by the Federal Reserve Bank of Kansas City, August 31–September 2, 1995, p. 269.

18. Ibid., pp. 269–271.

19. See, for example, *The Economic Report of the President*, February 1996, p. 105.

20. ''Long-Term Tendencies in Budget Deficits and Debt'' by Paul Masson and Michael Mussa in *Budget Deficits and Debt: Issues and Options*, a symposium sponsored by the Federal Reserve Bank of Kansas City, August 31–September 2, 1995, p. 36.

21. Assuming these deficit reductions are done gradually enough to avoid a recession. Recall that private investment is likely to be discouraged in a depressed economy even with lower interest rates. The impact of lower private investment could be a diminished future GDP.

22. See Chapter 3, Section 3.

6

Social Security, Medicare, and the Deficit

1. SOCIAL SECURITY AND MEDICARE: ARE THEY GOING BANKRUPT?

The baby boomers begin retiring in 2010, which will cause a huge drain on the Social Security and Medicare system. Many are worried these programs will become insolvent. The media are bombarding us with warnings. The *New Republic* recently had a cover showing a Social Security card with enormous letters saying "UH-OH." The caption read, "Social Security Is on the Skids. Does Anyone over 40 Give a Damn?" A December 1995 Gallup poll found that only 35% of Americans felt "fairly sure" that they could depend on their Social Security benefits.[1] Conventional wisdom holds that without drastic reforms our Social Security and Medicare trust funds will go bankrupt.

Is it true? What does it mean for a government trust fund to go bankrupt? How are these funds related to a budget deficit or surplus?

Government trust funds are widely misunderstood. According to the usual notion of a "trust fund," you pay in while you're working; your money is invested; and when you retire, you receive the fruits of your investment.[2]

Government trust funds are different. In fact, they are nothing more than an accounting technique to earmark certain revenues for specific programs.[3] The Social Security and Medicare (Hospital Insurance) Trust

Funds receive most of their money from the Social Security payroll (or FICA) tax.

Before 1983, Social Security was a pay-as-you-go system. That is, the money collected through payroll taxes on workers was handed over to retired beneficiaries. By the early 1980s, projections indicated that either the payroll tax would have to be increased or benefits would have to be cut in order for revenues to meet expenditures.

In 1983, a bipartisan presidential commission, headed by Alan Greenspan, recommended benefit cuts and payroll tax increases, which were quickly enacted by Congress.[4] Most important, the tradition of pay-as-you-go was abandoned. Instead, Social Security taxes were adjusted so that revenues would exceed benefits until the second decade of the twenty-first century. The surplus would accumulate in a trust fund reserve, consisting of U.S. government securities, which allegedly would help pay benefits to the upcoming generations. In mid-1996, these trust fund assets amounted to about $425 billion. They are projected to grow steadily until 2019, reaching $2.9 trillion.[5] After that they will be drawn down at a rapid rate, reaching zero in a decade. The Social Security Trust Fund is thus predicted to become "bankrupt" by 2029. After that date, the projected Social Security revenues will fund about 75% of benefits.

According to conventional accounting practice, the system could be restored to "actuarial soundness" by adjusting taxes and benefits so that the assets of the trust fund would not be depleted for 75 years.[6] This could be accomplished by raising the payroll tax by 2.2 percentage points (1.1 percent for employers and 1.1 percent for employees).[7]

Medicare costs are funded from two different sources. The first is the Hospital Insurance Trust Fund, the so-called Part A, which covers hospital care and is largely fed by the payroll tax. The second is the Medicare (Supplementary Medical Insurance) Trust Fund, which covers Part B services, like visits to private doctors. Part B is not financed by an earmarked tax. It receives most of its money from the Treasury's general fund, the revenues that keep most of the government operating.[8] By definition, the Part B Trust Fund does not run deficits or surpluses and can never go bankrupt. If Part B services have to be paid, the Treasury must come up with the money, either through taxing or borrowing.

Part A is the worry. While the Social Security Trust Fund will enjoy a growing surplus until 2019, the Medicare Part A Trust Fund is currently being depleted and is expected to go bankrupt around 2002.

In the spring of 1996, both President Clinton and the Republicans presented plans that purported to fend off bankruptcy in Part A until 2007.[9] The Republicans proposed curtailing spending by $123 billion over six years. The White House plan would have reduced spending by $72 billion over this period. In addition, in a tactic that the House Republicans had proposed in 1995, the president would have removed a portion of the cost of home health care, $55 billion, out of Part A and placed it in Part B, to be financed out of general revenues. These medical services would have remained the same, but the government would have paid for them out of a different pocket. As Robert Reischauer, former head of the CBO, put it, "You may call this a solution. I'd call it a rearrangement of the books."

As for Social Security, politicians of both parties have said that as of fall 1996, basic reforms are "off the table." As the saying goes, "Social Security is the third rail of American politics. Touch it and you're toast."

2. TRUST FUND BANKRUPTCY IS AN ILLUSION

What are the implications of bankruptcy for Social Security and Medicare? Probably not what you think.

The Social Security and Medicare Part A Trust Funds are required by law to invest any surplus in Treasury securities. In other words, one branch of government (the Treasury) is giving an IOU to another branch of the same government (the Social Security Administration). What does the Treasury do with the money it gets from the Social Security Administration? It uses the funds for authorized government purposes.[10]

As the economist Wallace Peterson put it:

tax money flowing into the Social Security Administration in excess of benefits paid is not really accumulated in a "fund" in a manner similar to the workings of private insurance. Any yearly surplus is invested in special interest-bearing government securities, which means the funds become a part of the general revenues of the government, to be spent for any legitimate government purpose.[11]

On this same point, listen to Peter Peterson:

Today's payroll taxes go directly from the pockets of today's workers straight to the mailboxes of today's retirees after a brief stop at the federal Treasury . . . any surplus of FICA taxes over benefits is "loaned" by Social Security to the Treasury, which uses the money to pay for other government programs.[12]

You frequently hear that the Treasury is "raiding the trust fund" by spending these surpluses. House Speaker Newt Gingrich put it this way:

The money the government supposedly has been putting aside from the baby boomers' Social Security taxes *is not there*. The government has been borrowing the money to pay for the budget deficit. So, when the baby boomers get set to retire, where's the money to pay them going to come from?[13]

The Treasury economist Francis X. Cavanaugh has argued that Gingrich's statement is "nonsense":

The fact that the money that goes into the trust fund is invested in Treasury securities and spent by the government does not mean that the trust fund has been looted. Other trust funds, private as well as public, invest in Treasury or other securities issued by borrowers who spend the borrowed money. Why else would they borrow? A real shocker would be a trust fund with money that is *not* invested and thus not producing earnings for the beneficiaries of the trust.[14]

Gingrich makes the more valid point. The money *really* isn't there. The Treasury took the money and ran, leaving behind a meaningless IOU earning meaningless interest. *A common misunderstanding about Social Security and Medicare is the notion that surpluses in these trust funds build up a stock of assets that can be used to finance benefits. This notion is false.* Let's see why.

Suppose the trust fund incurs a deficit. That is, its revenues are less than benefits. To raise the additional money, the fund will draw down its holdings of Treasury securities. It could obtain the money by selling these securities to the public, an action that would add to the budget deficit, since it involves government borrowing from the public. The only other possibility is for the Treasury to buy back these securities from the trust fund by raising the necessary taxes or by cutting other government spending.

By contrast, imagine that the trust fund is facing a deficit but with zero holdings of Treasury securities. That is, picture the fund as "bankrupt" as well as faced with benefits in excess of revenues. In this case the Treasury will have to raise the necessary money for the trust fund either by borrowing from the public or raising taxes or reducing other government spending.

Give yourself an A if you noticed that these options are identical to those when the trust fund is holding government assets. In other words, *trust fund assets are nothing more than an accounting fiction. If these assets are a fiction, so also is the notion of trust fund bankruptcy. You can't run out of something that is a nothing.* Fund assets may provide information about benefit and revenue trends. But it's a mistake to think they can be used to pay for anything. Is it really surprising that IOUs from one branch of the government to another should amount to anything but a zero?

Here is how Wallace Peterson explained this point:

When the Social Security Administration, which is a part of the government, presents these securities to the U.S. Treasury for redemption in order to pay Social Security benefits, where will the Treasury get the money? Taxes will have to be raised, or other spending cut[15] . . . or the budget deficit increased.

In Peter Peterson's words,

It's time to face up to the awful truth that trust-fund accounting is a hoax. . . .
A trust-fund ledger for such transfers [between the Social Security Administration and the Treasury] is a waste of time. Does it really help to know that Social Security is a bit richer and Treasury is a bit poorer? Given the apparent congressional appetite for constitutional amendments, why not consider one banning government trust funds?[16]

Imagine a family that used government trust fund accounting, earmarking a certain amount of its income for, say, medical expenses. If they incur medical expenses less than those earmarked, the family "borrows" the excess to spend on other things, leaving IOUs in place of the borrowed funds. Does the existence of these IOUs affect the family's ability to meet its future medical expenses? Of course not. Future expenses have to be met out of future income, and future income is unaffected by whether or not the family deposits an IOU with itself every time it spends part of its earmarked medical expenses for other things. To suppose that these IOUs can be used to pay for anything is an illusion. To label the absence of these IOUs as bankruptcy is also an illusion.

3. THE ECONOMIC IMPACT OF A TRUST FUND SURPLUS

If trust fund assets are a fiction, does that mean that the benefit cuts and the tax increases resulting from the Greenspan commission accomplished nothing? After all, the commission's recommendations did build up these phantom surpluses. Did their reforms help alleviate our projected budget crisis? Most economists would say yes. Cutting entitlements and raising the payroll tax depress the nation's consumption. In addition, creating a trust fund surplus meant that the Treasury could now ''borrow'' the fund's surplus to finance its expenditures, thereby reducing its borrowing from the public. Recall that a reduction in the budget deficit will normally cause the Fed to lower interest rates to prevent a recession, stimulating private investment and diminishing foreign indebtedness, both of which increase the nation's future income.[17] This was a central idea behind the commission's recommendations: to increase the nation's saving (investment at the expense of consumption), thereby boosting future GDP. Higher future income diminishes the burden on future workers of paying for entitlements. So while a trust fund surplus cannot directly be used to finance benefits, it can help indirectly by raising future GDP.

The fear of trust fund bankruptcy was an alarm bell that caused the politicians to embrace the Greenspan reforms. But, *raising taxes and cutting benefits would have had precisely the same impact on the economy if the trust fund had never existed.* Greenspan has reportedly made the same point by asserting that the only bottom line that really counts is the government's borrowing from the public.[18]

In 1990 there was a conference on the deficit at the University of Utah. Alan Blinder summarized the views of the participants. Here is what he said on Social Security and the deficit:

Many people are confused about the nature of the social security trust fund. Many people think of it as a kind of bank account into which they make ''deposits'' while they work so as to be able to make ''withdrawals'' when they retire. Nothing could be further from the truth. In fact, the fund is an accounting fiction. Most payroll taxes are used immediately to pay benefits to retirees. The rest is invested by law in U.S. securities—which is where the accounting fiction comes in.

The U.S. government is now running about a $150 billion overall deficit comprised of a $50 billion surplus in social security and a $200 billion in new bonds each year. But the social security trust fund buys $50 billion of them, which amounts to one branch of the government lending to another. Only $150 billion is left to be sold to private investors. . . .

Under the mainstream view [of economists], the large accumulation of funds in social security—that is, the large reduction of the national debt—will ease the burden of paying future social security benefits. How? Either it will:

1. lower interest rates and thereby raise investment, so there will be more capital and hence higher output per worker in the future.

2. limit our need for foreign borrowing, so that when the future rolls around, more U.S. assets will be owned by Americans.

In either case, the same payroll tax *rates* should generate more revenue.[19]

4. REFORMING SOCIAL SECURITY

A number of economists and politicians have suggested that a portion of the Social Security tax be invested in private securities, mainly stocks, with the hope that higher returns would help fund future benefits. The various privatization plans differ in the degree of control individuals would have over the investment of their Social Security taxes.

If privatization were to help our projected budget crisis, it would have to boost future GDP. Economists doubt that privatization would have such an effect.[20] As Olivia Mitchell and Stephen Zeldes conclude in their study of Social Security privatization, ''Overall, it seems precarious to build a case for privatization based on the argument that it would increase national saving.''

To understand the reasoning here, suppose the Social Security Trust Fund invests a part of its surplus in private securities instead of loaning it to the Treasury. The Treasury would now have to increase its borrowing from the public by the amount it no longer receives from the trust fund. While the government is lending funds to the private sector by purchasing private securities, it is at the same time borrowing a like sum. The two effects would likely cancel each other out in terms of the impact on private investment.[21]

As Dean Baker explains,

by itself, privatization cannot possibly make the economy grow faster. It just shifts around resources, requiring that individuals invest their social security taxes and the government borrow to make up the lost tax revenue. National saving is not increased one dollar.[22]

The economist Peter Diamond puts the same argument this way:

A number of proposals have been made to privatize some or all of Social Security

If other federal spending and revenue do not change, then we would expect no noticeable effect on the deficit or on national savings. . . .

Since the Treasury would have to borrow more from the public to offset decreased borrowing from Social Security, we are really inquiring about the effects of shifting Treasury borrowing from one source to another. I suspect that this "open market operation" would be close to a wash.[23]

Peter Peterson comes to the same conclusion:

If workers are simply allowed to shift their FICA taxes into savings accounts, the resulting increase in the federal deficit will cancel out the increase in private savings dollar for dollar. National savings—and future living standards—will be no better off than they would be if we had never reformed the system.[24]

If privatization schemes by themselves do not increase future GDP, what's the point? If people feel they own a personal investment account, they may be more willing to accept tax increases. As explained by Edward Gramlich, the chairman of the 1994 advisory council to the Social Security and Medicare Trustees,

individual accounts may increase individuals' sense of ownership of their Social Security rights; at present, the system must seem like a black box to most workers. . . .

The creation of mandatory individual accounts may represent a more politically acceptable way to raise national saving than by plain old rises in payroll tax rates. The individual accounts really are held on behalf of an individual as opposed to payroll taxes that largely finance current retirement benefits for someone else.[25]

It thus appears that a major purpose of privatization is to lessen the pain of raising taxes. Economists would classify this as a "good" type of deficit reduction or surplus increase, since hiking Social Security taxes would depress consumption, which could raise investment and thus increase future GDP.

NOTES

1. *Where America Stands* by Michael Golay and Carl Rollyson, p. 178.
2. *Economics*, 7th ed., by William Baumol and Alan Blinder, p. 474.
3. *The Economic and Budget Outlook: Fiscal Years 1997–2006*, May 1996, Congress of the United States, Congressional Budget Office, pp. 54–55.
4. *Economics*, 7th ed., by William Baumol and Alan Blinder, pp. 99–100.

5. "The Hard Facts about Social Security" by Olivia Mitchell and Joseph Quinn in *Challenge*, November–December, 1996, p. 17.

6. "Different Approaches for Dealing with Social Security" by Edward M. Gramlich in the *Journal of Economic Perspectives*, Summer 1996, p. 56.

7. "Restoring Social Security" by Lawrence Kotlikoff in *Challenge*, November–December 1996, p. 21.

8. The rest of the Part B trust fund money, 25%, comes from the monthly premium paid by those enrolled in the program.

9. See "Political Stakes Increase in Fight to Save Medicare" by Michael Wines, *New York Times*, June 3, 1996.

10. You often hear that surpluses in the Social Security Trust Fund should not be included in the official measure of the budget deficit. Such a claim is nonsense. Government trust fund surpluses or deficits must be included with other federal expenditures and revenues to obtain an accurate measure of the Treasury's borrowing from the public. As the CBO puts it: "The trust funds must be included in the budget totals with other programs when considering the effect of federal activities on national income and employment and on the Treasury's cash borrowing needs." *The Economic and Budget Outlook: Fiscal Years 1997–2006*, May 1996, Congress of the United States, Congressional Budget Office, p. 55.

11. *Silent Depression* by Wallace C. Peterson, p. 265.

12. *Will America Grow Up Before It Grows Old?* by Peter G. Peterson, pp. 47–48.

13. *The Truth about the National Debt* by Francis X. Cavanaugh, p. 98.

14. Ibid.

15. *Silent Depression* by Wallace C. Peterson, pp. 255–266.

16. *Will America Grow Up Before It Grows Old?* by Peter Peterson, pp. 47–48.

17. See Chapter 3, Section 2.

18. *Will America Grow Up Before It Grows Old?* by Peter Peterson, p. 48.

19. "Is the National Debt Really—I Mean, *Really*—a Burden?" by Alan Blinder in *Debt and the Twin Deficits Debate*, edited by James Rock, pp. 223–224.

20. "Different Approaches for Dealing with Social Security" by Edward M. Gramlich in the *Journal of Economic Perspectives*, Summer 1996, pp. 55–66. There were three approaches analyzed by the 1994 advisory council to the Social Security and Medicare trustees, chaired by Edward Gramlich. The first tried to maintain the present system as much as possible. It involves a tax increase on Social Security benefits combined with a direct investment by the Social Security Trust Fund in equities. The second decreases benefits and creates mandatory individual accounts. Individuals would have some choice about how these accounts would be invested. The individual's benefit on retirement would be the annuities on these accounts plus the regular Social Security benefit. The third

approach involves a tax increase along with a gradual replacement of the present system with large portions of the Social Security tax held outside the trust fund and placed in personal security accounts. The individual would have broad latitude as to how the funds in the accounts were to be used on retirement.

21. It is, of course, impossible to know for sure that privatization by itself will have no effect on national saving, one way or the other. Privatization could induce the government to change its expenditures or taxes. For example, investing part of the payroll tax in private securities would raise the measured budget deficit, even though the government's net borrowing from the public is unchanged. The higher measured deficit could cause the government to raise taxes or cut expenditures, which could raise national saving. Another possibility is that the private sector, being confronted with a different level of risk, could alter its saving, hence national saving. For example, if privatization made people feel more certain about their retirement benefits, their saving might fall, but the converse is also possible. For a discussion of these and other possibilities, see "Social Security Privatization: A Structure for Analysis" by Olivia S. Mitchell and Stephen P. Zeldes in *The American Economic Review*, May 1996, pp. 363–367.

22. "The Assumptions Are Too Pessimistic" by Dean Baker in *Challenge*, November–December 1996, p. 32.

23. "Proposals to Restructure Social Security" by Peter A. Diamond, in the *Journal of Economic Perspectives*, Summer 1996, pp. 72–73.

24. *Will America Grow Up Before It Grows Old?* by Peter Peterson, p. 135.

25. "Different Approaches for Dealing with Social Security" by Edward M. Gramlich in the *Journal of Economic Perspectives*, Summer 1996, pp. 60–61.

7

How Do European Countries Do It?

1. ZERO DEFICITS ARE NOT THE GOAL

Europeans view deficits differently than we do in the United States. Like us, they have become alarmed at recent increases in deficit spending. Unlike us, however, they are not attempting to balance their budgets. In Europe, public investment is widely acknowledged to be a legitimate reason for government borrowing.

This view is reflected in the 1991 Maastricht Treaty, which lays the foundation for a common European currency. To become a member of the European Monetary Union a country must limit its deficit to 3% and its national debt to 60% of GDP.

Why did the framers of the Maastricht Treaty concern themselves with the level of deficit spending? Why not let each country be responsible for its own fiscal policies? The architects of the treaty were concerned that one member's fiscal policy could have adverse effects on the others. Three of these effects have been emphasized.[1] First, if a country becomes unwilling to meet the interest payments on its debt, other countries could be forced to bail it out to avoid a financial panic. Anxiety over this possibility is so great that the treaty rules out any such bailout. Second, fear of a financial crisis resulting from a defaulting country could force the European Central Bank to purchase that country's debt, which could be inflationary.[2] Finally, excessive deficits could push up a country's interest rates, exerting upward pressure on the interest rates of other countries.

Why does the treaty limit deficit spending to 3% of GDP? Why not 1%? Why not 10%? Why not zero, as proposed for the United States? The 3% limit appears to be related to the "golden rule of public finance," namely, that borrowed funds should be used only for investment. The average public investment in the European Community from 1974 to 1991 was almost exactly 3% of GDP.[3] The golden rule is frequently referred to in European Community documents. Germany has enshrined this principle in its Constitution.[4]

Furthermore, the treaty specifies that the 3% limit could be relaxed if the borrowing were used for investment.[5]

Compare this European attitude toward borrowing with that in the United States, where federal borrowing is seen as evil no matter how the borrowed money is to be spent. In legitimating deficit spending for investment, the Maastricht Treaty appears to have implicitly recognized the distinction between a capital and a current budget, where the capital budget is characterized by borrowing for investment, while the current budget is expected to be balanced. This distinction between a capital and a current budget reflects the fiscal procedures of all the European countries. Unlike the United States, each of them provides separate measures of current and capital expenditures.[6]

There is another flexibility in the treaty's deficit target. The treaty states that a deficit above 3% might be allowed if "it is exceptional and temporary."[7] A reasonable interpretation of this wording is that deficits in excess of 3% might be allowable during a recession.[8] The treaty seems to acknowledge the consensus among economists that a cyclical deficit is beneficial because it serves as an automatic stabilizer.[9] By contrast, recent American proposals to balance the budget make no allowance for the automatic stabilizer. The balanced budget amendment to the Constitution, defeated in the Senate by one vote in March 1995, would have permitted deficits during a recession only if three-fifths of the members of both the House and the Senate voted to suspend the amendment's provisions.[10]

One criticism of the 3% rule is that it ignores inflation. If the treaty is designed to permit investment of 3% of GDP, then a deficit–GDP ratio of 3% is too low except under conditions of zero inflation. Inflation is projected to average 2% a year in Europe.[11] Recall that inflation causes the official deficit to overstate the real deficit, since part of the official deficit merely restores the inflation-eroded value of the public debt.[12]

Therefore, the deficit–GDP ratio would have to exceed 3% in order for public investment borrowing to equal 3% of GDP.[13] Given broadly accepted projections about inflation and output growth, a deficit–GDP ratio of 3% can be shown to imply public investment of only 1.8% of GDP.[14] To achieve investment of 3% of GDP would require a deficit–GDP ratio of 5%.[15]

By this logic, *our goal of balancing the budget actually implies a budget surplus*. Eliminating the 1995 U.S. deficit would have resulted in a *real* surplus of 1.4% of GDP.[16]

2. DEFICITS AND THE DEBT–GDP RATIO

Consider the other Maastricht criterion that the debt–GDP ratio should not exceed 60%.[17] Here also there is flexibility. If the debt–GDP ratio exceeds 60%, it will not be deemed excessive if it is "sufficiently diminishing and approaching the reference value at a satisfactory rate."[18] This exception is necessary because a number of European countries have debt–GDP ratios well in excess of 60%. In the cases of Belgium, Greece, and Italy, for example, this ratio currently exceeds 100%. There is little possibility that all the member countries could reach 60% by the target date of 1999.

Where did this magical 60% come from? It derives from the arithmetic of the deficit.[19] It can be shown that if the deficit–GDP ratio is maintained at 3%, the debt–GDP ratio will eventually reach 60%.[20] Thus, the two Maastricht fiscal norms are mutually consistent.

There is a common misperception that permanent deficits lead to an exploding burden of the debt (debt–GDP ratio). The arithmetic that links deficits and debt growth refutes this misperception. The truth is that *even permanently increasing deficits do not necessarily imply a growing debt burden*. (Note that maintaining the deficit at any fixed percent of GDP means that the deficit will increase at the same rate as the GDP.)

Running a yearly deficit that is a constant percent of GDP may cause the debt–GDP ratio to temporarily rise or fall, but in either case this ratio will eventually reach a stable value. For example, given broadly accepted assumptions about inflation and output growth in the United States,[21] maintaining our deficit at the 1995 level of 2.3% of GDP would cause the debt–GDP ratio to fall from the 1995 level of 50.2% to 46%.[22] If our deficit–GDP ratio were increased to 2.5%, the debt–GDP ratio would remain at around its current value of 50%. If our deficit–GDP

ratio were at 3%, the debt–GDP ratio would, as with Europe, eventually
stabilize at 60%.

3. HOW BIG CAN THE PUBLIC DEBT BE?

Is there any upper limit for the debt–GDP ratio? There is none that is
derivable from economics. The upper limit depends on the preferences
of the particular country, that is, how much public investment is valued
relative to the costs of the incurred debt.[23] This is one of the main crit-
icisms of the Maastricht criteria. Imposing the same numerical restrictions on several countries fails to take their differences into account. As
the economists Willem Buiter, Giancarlo Corsetti, and Nouriel Roubini
put it,

There is no case for restricting the debt–GDP to lie below any specific numerical
value; and a fortiori no case for an identical limit for 12 heterogeneous countries.[24]

A similar argument is made by the economists Paul Masson and Michael Mussa:

We do not have any theories that predict a precise upper limit for debt ratios.
Also, it is true of government debt that "we owe most of it to ourselves"; net
international indebtedness for industrial countries is generally a modest fraction
of total government debt.[25]

4. A DANGER OF DEFICIT TARGETS

Economists fear that attempts to reach these Maastricht norms will
lead to contractionary fiscal policies in several European countries. As
of 1994, those requiring the largest deficit reductions were Belgium,
Greece, Italy, and Sweden with debt–GDP ratios of 136%, 114%, 129%,
and 92%, respectively.[26] Even though the Maastricht requirements are
loosely worded, pressure on governments to raise taxes and reduce
spending could lead to a recession-prone Europe.

Buiter, Corsetti, and Roubini conclude,

Taking seriously Maastricht's transition to EMU [European Monetary Union]
will probably mean successive tax increases and spending cuts for the EC [Eur-
opean Community] as a whole. . . .

We conclude that the transition to EMU is likely to be deflationary in the EC. Three independent model simulations . . . support this conclusion. . . .

for countries requiring major deficit reductions, the effect on economic activity is negative, despite interest rate cuts.[27]

The same worry holds with even greater force for the United States, since an aversion to deficits is much harsher than the loose European deficit target.

NOTES

1. See *The Commission of the European Communities*, 1991, chapter on public finance.

2. Such actions by the European Central Bank would increase the European money supply and could, as a result, cause inflation.

3. "Excessive Deficits: Sense and Nonsense in the Treaty of Maastricht," by Willem Buiter, Giancarlo Corsetti, and Nouriel Roubini in *Economic Policy: A European Forum*, April 1993, p. 63, and "European versus American Perspectives on Balanced-Budget Rules" by Giancarlo Corsetti and Nouriel Roubini in *The American Economic Review*, May 1996, p. 409.

4. "Excessive Deficits: Sense and Nonsense in the Treaty of Maastricht," by Willem Buiter, Giancarlo Corsetti, and Nouriel Roubini in *Economic Policy: A European Forum*, April 1993, p. 98.

5. The treaty states that if deficits exceed the 3% norm, consideration will be given to "whether the government deficit exceeds government investment expenditures." Ibid., p. 61.

6. See "European versus American Perspectives on Balanced-Budget Rules" by Giancarlo Corsetti and Nouriel Roubini in *The American Economic Review*, May 1996, p. 409.

7. Ibid.

8. Corsetti and Roubini point out that this interpretation is also supported by the wording of Article 104c, which refers to the "medium term . . . budgetary position of the Member State" as being relevant to whether or not the deficit is excessive. That is, if deficits are incurred during recessions, they should be eliminated as the economy recovers and become surpluses if the economy becomes inflationary.

9. For an explanation of the automatic (cyclical) deficit, see Chapter 2, Section 6.

10. This balanced budget amendment was passed easily in the House by 300 to 116.

11. "Excessive Deficits: Sense and Nonsense in the Treaty of Maastricht,"

by Willem Buiter, Giancarlo Corsetti, and Nouriel Roubini in *Economic Policy: A European Forum*, April 1993, p. 63.

12. For an explanation of how inflation causes the official deficit to exaggerate the real deficit, see Chapter 2, Section 10.

13. The basic formula is that the rate of change in the debt–GDP ratio equals the deficit–GDP ratio minus the debt–GDP ratio times the growth rate in dollar (nominal) GDP. It follows that, at the stable debt–GDP ratio, the deficit–GDP ratio must equal the growth rate in nominal GDP times the debt–GDP ratio. The growth rate in nominal GDP is equal to the inflation rate plus the growth rate in real (inflation-adjusted) GDP. Subtracting from the deficit the inflation rate times the debt gives the real deficit. Therefore, the real deficit–GDP ratio equals the growth rate in real GDP times the debt–GDP ratio. It follows that maintaining an investment–GDP ratio of 3%, with a projected inflation rate of 2% and a real GDP growth rate of 3%, can be shown to imply convergence to a debt–GDP ratio of 100% and a deficit–GDP ratio of 5%. Maintaining a lower public investment–GDP ratio of, say, 2% would imply a stable debt–GDP ratio of 67% and a deficit–GDP ratio of 3.3%.

14. A 3% deficit–GDP ratio would cause the debt–GDP ratio to stabilize at 60%. Given the latter ratio, a 2% inflation rate would imply that the real value of the public debt would decrease by 1.2% (2% of 60%) of GDP. Thus, *real* government borrowing for investment would be 1.8% of GDP (3% minus 1.2%).

15. A 5% deficit–GDP ratio would cause the debt–GDP ratio to stabilize at 100%. Given the latter ratio, a 2% inflation rate would imply that the real value of the public debt would decrease by 2% (2% of 100%) of GDP. Thus, *real* government borrowing for investment would be 3% of GDP (5% minus 2%).

16. In 1995, the U.S. inflation rate was around 2.7%, and the debt–GDP ratio was approximately 50%. Therefore, 2.7% of 50% constituted the fraction of GDP that equaled the erosion in the purchasing power of the public debt. This number was around $100 billion. The official U.S. deficit that year was $164 billion. Of this official deficit, around $100 billion was therefore not *real* borrowing; it was that portion of the issuance of new government debt that simply restored the real value of the public debt. Consequently, only the remaining $64 billion constituted the *real* deficit. Eliminating the official deficit of $164 billion, therefore, would imply a *real* surplus of $100, which was about 1.4% of the GDP (of $7.18 trillion). Data were obtained from *The Economic and Budget Outlook: Fiscal Years 1997–2006*, May 1996, Congress of the United States, Congressional Budget Office.

17. For some reason, the treaty's guidelines apply to gross public debt rather than the more relevant net debt. The gross debt includes the government debt held by some branch of the government itself, such as the central bank. For a discussion of this point, see ''Excessive Deficits: Sense and Nonsense in the Treaty of Maastricht'' by Willem Buiter, Giancarlo Corsetti, and Nouriel Rou-

bini in *Economic Policy: A European Forum*, April 1993, pp. 73–74. See also the Introduction, Section 3.

18. "European versus American Perspectives on Balanced-Budget Rules" by Giancarlo Corsetti and Nouriel Roubini in *The American Economic Review*, May 1996, p. 409.

19. For the basic formula, see note 13.

20. Assuming the nominal GDP grows at the annual average rate of 5%, which is the projected rate for Europe. If, for example, the nominal GDP growth rate increased to, say, 6%, due to either faster inflation or faster growth in real GDP, then a maintained 3% deficit–GDP ratio would imply convergence to a debt–GDP ratio of 50%.

21. See *The Economic and Budget Outlook: Fiscal Years 1997–2006*, May 1996, Congress of the United States, Congressional Budget Office, p. 15.

22. This assumes a growth rate of nominal GDP of 5%. If, however, the projected growth rate in nominal GDP were, say, 6%, because of either a higher inflation rate or a faster growth rate in real GDP, then a maintained deficit–GDP ratio of the current 2.3% would lead to a decline in the debt–GDP ratio from the current value of 50.2% to 38.3%.

23. The costs of the public debt consist of the tax cost of servicing the debt plus, in a full-employment economy, the value of the private investment crowded out as a result of the public borrowing. In a depressed economy, public investment would increase employment and likely stimulate private investment. See Chapter 2.

24. "Excessive Deficits: Sense and Nonsense in the Treaty of Maastricht" by Willem Buiter, Giancarlo Corsetti, and Nouriel Roubini in *Economic Policy: A European Forum*, April 1993, p. 87.

25. "Long-Term in Budget Deficits and Debt" by Paul Masson and Michael Mussa in *Budget Deficits and Debt: Issues and Options*, a symposium sponsored by the Federal Reserve Bank of Kansas City, August 31–September 2, 1995, p. 29.

26. Ibid., p. 30, Table 5.

27. "Excessive Deficits: Sense and Nonsense in the Treaty of Maastricht" by Willem Buiter, Giancarlo Corsetti, and Nouriel Roubini in *Economic Policy: A European Forum*, April 1993, p. 76. For a similar argument, see "Fiscal Discipline and the Budget Process" by Alberto Alesina and Roberto Perotti in *The American Economic Review*, May 1996, pp. 401–407. They also criticize numerical targets for increasing the incentives for "creative and non-transparent accounting" (p. 402).

8

Goal '95: A Balanced Budget by 2002

What I've tried to do in this book is to give you, the reader, a rational way to think about a deficit or a surplus. By contrast, political discussion of the deficit has been anything but rational. Let's look at a case study of how a decision about the deficit was actually made by our political leaders. Precious little sound economic reasoning was evident. It appears that the criterion for selecting policy was more image than substance.

1. THE REPUBLICANS EMBRACE A BALANCED BUDGET

In 1981, in testimony before the House Budget Committee, Congressman Jack Kemp, a respected, conservative Republican, said, "We Republicans no longer worship at the altar of a balanced budget."[1] In his speech before the Republican National Convention of 1996, vice presidential candidate Jack Kemp declared, "Our first step will be to balance the budget."

The Republicans have clearly returned to the altar. Even though the deficit steadily declined from 1992 through 1995; even though five-year deficit-reduction packages were passed in both 1990 and 1993, reducing cumulative deficits by over $900 billion[2]; even though both Congress and the White House were already committed to bringing the deficit down further, yet, in 1995 the Republican-controlled Congress adopted the goal of completely eliminating the deficit in seven years.

True, the Republicans had long advocated a constitutional amendment to balance the budget. But this was different. As the economist Herb Stein pointed out, if the balanced budget amendment had actually passed in Congress in 1995, the pressure on the Republicans to eliminate the deficit might have been less, since "they could have basked in their accomplishment as budget balancers, without having to do anything more for a while."[3]

Now they meant business. They were actually presenting concrete budget proposals to bring about a zero deficit. How did this policy change come about?

Reports by Elizabeth Drew and others indicate that the Speaker of the House, Newt Gingrich, acting virtually alone, spearheaded the movement to balance the budget by 2002.[4] As Drew explains it, "Gingrich had figured out that talking about 'balancing the budget' was easier to rally people than saying 'lower the deficit.' "[5]

Listen to Gingrich:

People will take a much higher level of discomfort if the end result is a zero, that they are literally going to quit piling debt on their children. In other words, if we're going to pile fifty billion dollars a year onto the deficit, you'll take dramatically less discomfort than if I say we're going to balance the budget. You actually get more, dramatically more, I think, by going for zero.[6]

Gingrich's decision to go "for zero" caught the Republican leadership by surprise. Republican congressman John Kasich, the chairman of the House Budget Committee, had been advocating only deficit reduction, not elimination, labeling it as a "down payment" on a balanced budget. He reacted to Gingrich's 2002 deadline by saying, "Is this really written in stone?"[7] As an unnamed "leadership aide" described it,

It was Newt way out there on his own. The Senate had not bought into this yet. All he had was almost a flip vote in the House leadership the day before (on February 15, 1995)—it wasn't like there was a big deliberate discussion of the question—but he announced the policy publicly the next day so that nobody could backtrack from it.[8]

Republican Senator Pete Domenici, chairman of the Senate Budget Committee, was also caught by surprise. Elizabeth Drew describes what happened:

Pete Domenici, dubious about the idea of trying to actually balance the budget by 2002, for some time after the election ascribed the House Republican leaders' setting that goal to their unfamiliarity with the arithmetic and set his own goal of making "a down payment" on a balanced budget. At an evening meeting in February, Domenici was taken aback by comments by both House and Senate leaders about their intention of not just winning approval of a Balanced Budget Amendment but of also actually balancing the budget. "I thought we were talking about a down payment," Domenici said. He felt that some important decisions had been made that he hadn't been party to. By the time the Balanced Budget Amendment failed in the Senate by one vote, Domenici knew that the Republicans were now so far out on a limb on balancing the budget—and on responding to Democratic taunts that they couldn't do it—that he would have to try to do so.[9]

2. PRESIDENT CLINTON SUCCUMBS

Like the Republicans, the Democrats had been advocating deficit reduction, not deficit elimination. But in June 1995, President Clinton had a change of heart. He explained his reasoning to his cabinet by saying, "The ticket to admission to American politics is a balanced budget."[10] Up to that moment he had fought the idea. He first responded to the Republicans by proposing to balance the budget in ten years, but he eventually agreed to Gingrich's original demand of seven years.

Many Democrats were angry that President Clinton had given in to the Republicans.[11] Vice President Al Gore was reportedly upset.[12] Clinton's chief economic adviser, Laura Tyson, felt there was no acceptable way to do it.[13] David Obey, the ranking Democrat on the House Budget Committee said, "If you can follow this White House on the budget, you are a whole lot smarter than I am."[14]

3. PROPOSED CUTS TO BALANCE THE BUDGET

To the politicians, a zero-deficit target may be a rallying cry or a reaction to taunts or a ticket of admission, but the human implications are serious. Consider how far the Congress went in the budget proposal it adopted in May 1995.[15]

- The Earned Income Tax Credit for the working poor was cut.
- Medicaid, which provides medical assistance to low-income people, was turned into a block grant, and its funding was reduced.

- The House reduced Medicare by $288 billion, and the Senate by $256 billion.
- Substantial cuts were made in education and training programs.
- Clinton's national service program (AmeriCorps) was eliminated. The volunteers in this program are paid to work with local governments or charities.
- Government loans for college education were reduced.
- The House eliminated, and the Senate cut, the funding for Clinton's Goals 2000, designed to encourage schools to attain higher standards.
- The Office of Technology Assessment, a nonpartisan think tank and the source of "studies for Congress on subjects ranging from the technical realities of nuclear proliferation to the economics of prostate cancer screening,"[16] was abolished.

Here is how the columnist David Broder evaluated these cuts:

A plan (the Earned Income Tax Credit) that has enjoyed bipartisan support for 20 years, as a way of encouraging people to leave welfare for entry-level jobs and helping keep families out of poverty while they work their way up is being jeopardized in the name of reducing the deficit. . . .

Contrary to what we would like to believe, the vital effort to get the budget back in balance is not an evenhanded, share-and-share-alike endeavor, but one that hits hardest on the most economically vulnerable and politically defenseless people in our society—poor women and children. . . .

The savings projected in low-income programs like Medicaid, welfare and food stamps in the current Republican budget are seven times the size of those passed in Ronald Reagan's first Congress. . . .

These low income programs take 45 percent of the entitlement reductions . . . —almost twice their proportional share.[17]

Here is another assessment from *Newsweek* reporter Marc Levinson:

The six-lane Woodrow Wilson Bridge between Virginia and Maryland has become an all-day traffic jam operating at more than twice its capacity. Replacing the crumbling federally owned bridge would cost up to $2 billion, and Congress is unlikely to approve. That's fine for the budget. But for the economy, it's not so hot. Shippers, truckers and commuters pay every day for blockages of the East coast's main artery.

Early evidence is that some of the budget busting is self-defeating. Balancing the budget is meant to unleash (private) investment that will kick the economy onto a higher plane. But to make their numbers, congressional Republicans have targeted government investments in transport, science and education. Says Robert Reischauer, until recently the head of the Congressional Budget Office, "If that's what turns out to be, watch out."[18]

4. CLINTON'S ECONOMISTS ON THE BALANCED BUDGET

Although President Clinton endorsed the goal of balancing the budget by 2002, I failed to find any support for this policy in the *1996 Economic Report of the President*, written by his own economic advisers.[19] Economist James Galbraith had the same experience.[20] He commented that the Council of Economic Advisors "says not one word about the benefits of a zero-deficit target, and for the obvious reason, I think, that no such benefits exist."

President Clinton's economists not only refrained from defending his balanced-budget goal but used a lot of ink condemning the "wrong" kinds of deficit reduction. They were worried that the rush to balance the budget would hurt our children. For example,

Deficit reduction done the wrong way will reduce living standards. . . .

Reducing the deficit should lower interest rates and stimulate private investment. Cutting the deficit by cutting high-return *public* investments makes little sense: it merely substitutes one worthwhile investment for another. Indeed, deficit reduction that reduces high-return public investments—like those in research and development, technology, education, and training—may compromise long-term economic growth.[21]

5. AN ARGUMENT FOR A BALANCED BUDGET

Are there any arguments in support of zeroing out the deficit? While our political leaders haven't presented substantive rationales for a balanced budget, some academics and columnists have. The reasoning stems from the Nobel Prize-winning economist James Buchanan.[22] He argues that the cost of deficits is invisible. Since everyone likes lower taxes and more government services, there will be a bias toward excessive deficits. Therefore, unless there is an ironclad rule that the budget must be balanced, politicians will succumb to the lure of deficits, appropriate or not.[23]

Robert Samuelson, a national columnist for *Newsweek* and the *Washington Post*, is one of the commentators who endorses Buchanan's idea:

Until the 1960s, the informal belief in the virtue of a balanced budget created a discipline that, if not fostering an explicit public philosophy, at least compelled a crude calibration of the costs and benefits of new government spending. Was the potential gain worth the pain of extra taxes? Once budget deficits became routine, even this discipline vanished. [Deficits] have been the path of least resistance, and it's easy to see why. Raising taxes isn't easy. Neither is cutting spending.[24]

Perhaps James Buchanan and Robert Samuelson are right that the cost of deficits is invisible; that voters will consequently pressure politicians to overspend and undertax; and that the solution is to tie the government's hands with a balanced-budget amendment. The key premise here is that the average citizen is unable to fathom the cost of deficits. If that's true, why is there such a furor over the deficit? To me, the opposite seems closer to the truth: people are irrationally averse to deficits.

Moreover, if Buchanan and Samuelson can understand the cost and benefits of deficits, why not the general public? As Robert Samuelson explains it:

arguably, the long-run effects of persistent deficits could be either good or bad. They might "crowd out" private investment, undermining future living standards. . . . On the other hand, productive government spending (on, say, education or research and development) might conceivably raise the economy's long-term growth.[25]

Is this reasoning too difficult for the American public? I don't believe it.

If deficits can be good or bad, as Samuelson asserts, why not support the good and oppose the bad? Samuelson's answer is that "claims and counterclaims of all sorts can be made, and none can easily be judged, because the consequences—whatever they might be—are usually lodged in the hazy future."[26]

No doubt the future is uncertain. But does it follow we should do away with borrowing? Why not rely on our best judgment instead of binding ourselves to an arbitrary rule of thumb that precludes borrowing no matter what the project? Consider private investments, such as a corporation building a plant or a student borrowing money for higher education. The consequences of these actions are also lodged in the "hazy future." Both the plant and the student may fail. But no one says that corporations and students should never borrow.

Samuelson even emphasizes, and correctly so, that the free market is not infallible and that private investment is often wasteful:

Poor investment, rather than low investment, may have undermined growth. In the 1980s, there was huge over investment in office buildings, hotels, and shopping centers. . . . Ordinary corporate investment is also often wasteful. In the 1980s IBM and General Motors, to take two examples, invested vast amounts in what turned out to be unneeded factories.[27]

But Samuelson doesn't infer from this wasted investment that the private sector should eliminate borrowing. Only the federal government.

6. BALANCE THE BUDGET? YES, THE OPERATING BUDGET!

Other columnists have different views about budget balancing. Listen to Molly Ivins, whose argument summarizes a major theme of this book:

Look, borrowing money is not bad. Families do it, companies do it and governments do it. The knot heads making this case keep insisting: "But the states have to balance their budgets; they can't run a deficit." Bull. The states balance their *operating* budgets. Texas borrows money all the time by floating bond issues—how do you think we're paying for all those ungodly expensive new prison cells? Did you ever vote on a school bond issue? Ever hear of a bond issue for a new sewage treatment plant?

As far as I know, no one government has ever had to balance both its capital and its operating budgets. Capital budgets have always been considered investments. Schools, universities, laboratories, even job-training programs don't produce benefits for years—just as families borrow money to finance a home or a college education. Presumably, both your home and your college education will end up being worth more than you paid for them.[28]

The *Washington Post* columnist E. J. Dionne, Jr., argues that chronic deficits and escalating health and pension costs have reduced the government to a "caretaker role" with little chance to undertake needed public investments, a situation that helps explain the American people's frustration with government. He also urges a capital budget:

Government needs to rediscover its dynamic role as an investor in growth. One approach . . . argues that the federal government should divide its budget between "consumption" and "investment" spending. Except during sharp economic downturns, it makes good sense to balance the consumption budget. Debt is most useful as a way of financing necessary investments that pay off in the long term—which is why cities and states float bond issues for roads, schools, highways and environmental projects, and why businesses sell bonds to build plants and buy equipment. The current deficit argument is a dead end because it treats all government spending as the same, much as if an individual treated the purchase of expensive restaurant meals and investments in a home or a business as being equivalent uses of money.[29]

Here is what the economist Robert Heilbroner had to say about the goal of balancing the budget:

A blanket injunction against federal borrowing might cause the government to eliminate waste, but it would also make public investment impossible.
   That would mean good-bye to such improvements as bridges, tunnels, highways, public-health research centers and other undertakings that would normally be considered public-sector business but could not be financed by taxation, because, as is the case with mortgages and business capital expenditures, the outlay is too large to be charged against one year's income.[30]

In March 1995, as President Clinton was pondering how to react to the balanced budget agenda of the Republicans, labor secretary Robert Reich reportedly urged the same advice on the president that I would have.

Reich had privately urged the President that if he felt compelled to respond to the movement toward a balanced budget in Congress he not only should delay such a response, but also consider the idea of moving to a capital budget, in which investments in future productivity aren't counted as current expenditures. Reich tried to convince Clinton—he had been trying for some time—that this would be consistent with his "investment" strategy (investing in education and training and infrastructure) and would be easy to explain to the public. As Reich explained it, "It's about spending for a European vacation or for your child's college education" or "business borrows for expensive machinery if there is likely to be a healthy return on investment." But Clinton had tried in vain, if sporadically, for two years to get across the "investment" idea, and felt there had been little return for his efforts.[31]

I would have added one thing to Reich's reported advice. Along with the capital budget, institute procedural changes that safeguard against the danger that a capital budget would be used as an excuse for pork-barrel projects.[32]

Recently, one of my colleagues who had just returned from Europe said to us over lunch, "It sure was nice to be in countries where the debates about economics are sensible."

NOTES

1. *Balanced Budgets and American Politics* by James D. Savage, p. 210.

2. See *Reducing the Deficit: Spending and Revenue Options*, the Congress of the United States, Congressional Budget Office, February 1995, p. 1.

3. *They Only Look Dead* by E. J. Dionne, Jr., p. 225.

4. Ibid., p. 224; *Tell Newt to Shut Up* by David Maraniss and Michael Weisskopf (New York: Touchstone, 1996), pp. 37–38.

5. *Showdown* by Elizabeth Drew, p. 85.

6. Ibid., p. 85.

7. Ibid., p. 128; *Tell Newt to Shut Up* by David Maraniss and Michael Weisskopf, p. 38.

8. *Showdown* by Elizabeth Drew, pp. 128–129.

9. Ibid., pp. 203–204; *They Only Look Dead* by E. J. Dionne, Jr., pp. 22–230.

10. *Showdown* by Elizabeth Drew, p. 234.

11. *They Only Look Dead* by E. J. Dionne, Jr., p. 284.

12. *Showdown* by Elizabeth Drew, pp. 346, 349.

13. Ibid., p. 338.

14. Ibid., p. 237.

15. Ibid., pp. 208–209.

16. See "Endangered Expertise" by Daniel Greenberg in *The Washington Post Weekly*, August 21–27, 1995. He is the editor and publisher of *Science and Government Report*, a Washington newsletter.

17. *Washington Post*, October 2, 1995.

18. *Newsweek*, June 5, 1995, pp. 45–46.

19. The economists responsible for the *1996 Economic Report of the President* are Joseph Stiglitz of Stanford University, Martin Baily of University of Maryland, and Alicia Munnell, director of research at the Federal Reserve Bank of Boston.

20. See "The Economic Report of the President, February 1996: A Review" in *Challenge*, May–June 1996, pp. 53–57. The quote is on p. 55.

21. *The Economic Report of the President*, February 1996, p. 37.

22. *Democracy in Deficit: The Political Legacy of Lord Keynes* by James Buchanan and Richard Wagner.

23. For a discussion, see *Economic Politics: The Costs of Democracy* by William Keech, pp. 29–30.

24. *The Good Life and Its Discontents* by Robert Samuelson, pp. 156–57.

25. Ibid., p. 166.

26. Ibid.

27. Ibid., pp. 132–133.

28. *Raleigh News and Observer*, March 2, 1995.

29. *They Only Look Dead* by E. J. Dionne Jr., pp. 285–286.

30. *New York Times*, March 2, 1995.

31. *Showdown* by Elizabeth Drew, p. 223.

32. Such as designating a respected and nonpartisan organization, like the CBO, to separate the pork from legitimate public investments.

9

Deficit Myths: What's True, What's False?

False and frightening notions have grown up like a jungle around the truth about the deficit, fed by news stories, editorials, television reports, and political speeches. To hack through this jungle and throw light on the truth are no easy task. People have become upset and even angry when I challenged their mistaken convictions about the deficit.

In this chapter, I examine the following assertions:

- We must pay off the public debt.
- Deficits can bankrupt our government.
- Deficits cause inflation.
- Deficits increase interest rates.
- Interest on the public debt will impoverish future generations.
- Budget deficits cause trade deficits.
- Deficits cause capital flight.
- Deficits increase the tax burden of future generations.
- The public debt will reduce our children's standard of living.
- Deficits crowd out private investment.
- Interest on the public debt crowds out other government spending
- The solution is a balanced budget amendment to the Constitution.

Although widely believed to be true, each of these allegations is either false or valid only under special circumstances. I will identify the grain of truth in each statement (when there is one).

MYTH 1. WE MUST PAY OFF THE PUBLIC DEBT

How often have you heard politicians present their calculations of the public debt "owed" by each of us, with a warning that we will have to "settle up" some day? The truth is that *a nation, unlike a family, never has to pay off its debt, and no nation has ever done so.* Each time the principal comes due, the U.S. Treasury simply "rolls it over." That is, new debt is issued to pay off the old. The U.S. Treasury does this all the time, weekly, in fact.

The government, unlike an individual or family, can be in debt forever. Why? Because the government doesn't die. Lenders may be reluctant to extend long-term credit to the elderly, since their heirs can't be forced to pay, but this collection risk does not exist when we lend money to the government by buying government securities.

In this respect the government is like a corporation. Corporations don't pay off their debt either. Like the government, they roll it over.

MYTH 2. DEFICITS CAN BANKRUPT OUR GOVERNMENT

A typical example of this myth appeared in an editorial in our local paper, the *Raleigh News and Observer*, which argued that we should reduce the deficit in order "to help restore the government to solvency."[1]

The notion that deficits can bankrupt our government is based on a false analogy between the government and a private debtor, such as a family or a business. If private debtors borrow too much, they become "insolvent," that is, unable to pay off their creditors. Could the same thing happen to our federal government? No.

There are two reasons we needn't fear that our government will default on its debt. First, we have a stable government with the power to raise revenue by taxation if necessary. Second and most important, U.S. debt is an obligation to pay in U.S. dollars, and since the U.S. Constitution gives the federal government the authority to create these dollars, the government can always pay off its creditors. This constitutional authority is an ironclad guarantee to investors that they will never face default on a U.S. government security. Not every country is in such an enviable position. Argentina, Brazil, and Mexico, for example, have debts that call for payment in U.S. dollars.

Does it sound irresponsible to talk about printing money to pay off our debt? Does it raise the specter of rampant inflation and double-digit interest rates? Read on.

MYTH 3. DEFICITS CAUSE INFLATION

It is true that incurring a deficit boosts spending. Whether the increased spending triggers inflation depends on the state of the economy and the reaction of the Fed. If the economy is depressed, and unemployment is widespread, an increase in total demand is unlikely to be inflationary.[2] Since a stagnant economy has idle labor and unutilized productive capacity, additional spending will increase production rather than prices.

If employment is high, an increase in total spending will probably push up prices. Even in this situation, however, incurring a deficit need not trigger inflation. To offset the increase in deficit spending, the Fed, our protector against inflation, will drive up interest rates to prevent an upsurge in total spending. If the Fed is successful, inflation will be avoided.

If the deficit increases too quickly or too much in a high-employment economy, the Fed may be unable to contain total spending. Under these circumstances, the deficit may cause inflation.[3] This is the grain of truth in the myth.

MYTH 4. DEFICITS INCREASE INTEREST RATES

In the first presidential debate of 1984, Walter Mondale argued that "everybody, every economist, every businessman" agrees that deficits increase interest rates.

Here is the logic behind this myth: a deficit means that the U.S. Treasury is borrowing funds from the public. Borrowing by so prominent a borrower will push up the cost of borrowing—interest rates.

So far so good. But this reasoning ignores the role of the major player in the Treasury securities market, the Fed. The Fed has the legal authority to buy and sell as many government securities as necessary to determine interest rates.[4] If the Fed sees inflation looming, it will push up interest rates to curb total spending. If the Fed fears a recession, it will lower interest rates to stimulate demand. *The Fed operates in this manner what-*

ever is happening to the deficit. For this reason, a rising deficit could be accompanied by either rising or falling interest rates. For example, the deficit increased during the early 1980s and again during the early 1990s. Interest rates rose during the earlier period but fell during the later period.

MYTH 5. INTEREST ON THE PUBLIC DEBT WILL IMPOVERISH FUTURE GENERATIONS

Deficits add to the public debt—the stock of government securities held by the public. These securities can be purchased by foreigners as well as U.S. citizens. Debt held by foreigners is called *external debt.* Domestically held debt is called *internal debt.*

Interest payments on the internal debt can't impoverish future generations. This debt requires taxing one group of Americans to make payments to another group of Americans. Our income is redistributed but not lost.

External debt is another matter. External debt *does* involve a cost to future generations. As the debt is paid, U.S. goods are sacrificed. They are transferred to foreign countries. Is this a reason to refrain from borrowing from foreign countries? Not at all. As with any borrowing, the key question is: Will the funds be put to profitable enough use to justify the cost? If so, the borrowing will generate sufficient future income to pay off the debt with something left over. In this case, external debt could be beneficial for our children.

Deficits and external debt can vary independently of each other, as I explain in the next myth.

MYTH 6. BUDGET DEFICITS CREATE TRADE DEFICITS

In the Introduction I referred to a Herblock cartoon showing the budget deficit as a Frankenstein monster with "MADE IN USA" tattooed on its forehead. What I didn't mention was that beside the monster is his little brother, a smaller version of Frankenstein labeled "trade deficit." The cartoon reflects the conventional wisdom that budget deficits are always accompanied by trade deficits.[5] (A trade deficit is an excess of imports over exports. We must pay for this excess by borrowing from foreigners, that is, by incurring external debt.)

In this case conventional wisdom is not correct. A budget deficit need not add to our external debt. The higher our interest rates, the more attractive our securities to foreign investors, which increases our external debt. But deficits can be associated with either rising or falling interest rates, as explained in Myth 4. Thus, *a growing deficit may be associated with either an increase or a decrease in our external debt.*

To illustrate, during the recession of 1981–1982, our interest rates and our deficit both increased, as did our external debt. But during the recession of 1990–1992, our deficit grew while interest rates and foreign indebtedness both fell.[6]

MYTH 7. DEFICITS CAUSE CAPITAL FLIGHT

Many worry that chronic budget deficits will cause foreigners to get spooked by our growing national debt and pull out of U.S. assets with dire consequences for our economy.

Is a flight from the dollar a reasonable fear? Most economists believe it's not. They see such a scenario (referred to as a "hard landing") as a most remote possibility, even with the huge deficits of recent years. As Lawrence Ball and Gregory Mankiw observe in their recent study of budget deficits, "As far as we know, no major industrialized country has ever experienced a hard landing."[7] Alberto Giovanni concludes from his research, "The arguments against [a] hard landing appear to be overwhelming."[8] Robert Heilbroner and Peter Bernstein also dismiss the likelihood of a flight from the dollar: "Suffice it to say that foreigners will continue to want to hold dollar assets as long as Americans want to hold dollar assets—as long, that is, as we maintain an economic environment congenial to enterprise. That seems like a sound bet."[9]

Nevertheless, for any number of reasons, investors could elect to shift their funds into other currencies.[10] They could, for example, develop doubts about the soundness of the U.S. economy because of our deficits or even because we are attempting to balance the budget.

For whatever reason, suppose capital did flee the United States. Would that be a disaster for us? Hardly. Not unless the Fed became paralyzed at the same time. Capital flight would put upward pressure on our interest rates and drive down the value of our dollar. The Fed would hold our interest rates steady, but the value of our dollar would likely fall, cheapening our exports and making our imports more expensive. A depreciating dollar would shrink our trade deficit, which, in fact, many would see as a benefit for the United States.

The value of the dollar does fluctuate, and whenever any price varies, there are winners and losers. But we're not talking disaster. As Paul Krugman summed it up,

If foreigners lose confidence in the United States, the immediate impact will be a fall in the dollar. But so what? From early 1985 to early 1987 the dollar lost roughly half its value in terms of the yen and the mark. Yet, this slow-motion financial crash did no more damage than the fast-forward fall in stock prices that followed. Unemployment continued to decline and inflation accelerated only slightly.[11]

A final point: if foreigners did dump dollars, market forces would automatically be activated that would dissipate their dumping urge. The decline in the value of the dollar would cheapen American assets, thus making them more attractive to foreigners.

MYTH 8. DEFICITS INCREASE THE TAX BURDEN OF FUTURE GENERATIONS

Deficits add to the public debt and to the interest payments on that debt and therefore increase our future taxes. Higher taxes, however, do not necessarily imply a greater tax *burden*. To gauge a tax burden, we must consider not only our taxes but our ability to pay those taxes.

How do deficits affect our future tax burden? That depends on how the government spends the borrowed funds. If the government invests in projects that improve our future income, our tax burden could fall. (Among public investments that could reduce the future tax burden are education, infrastructure, and research and development.[12])

For example, deficits could increase your daughter's annual taxes from $10,000 to $11,000 but cause her annual income to rise from $30,000 to $40,000. Such an outcome would reduce her future tax burden from 33.3% to 27.5%.

If the government runs a deficit and uses the borrowed money for consumption—Social Security or congressional salaries, for example—then our future tax burden could increase, since consumption does not increase future income.[13]

MYTH 9. THE PUBLIC DEBT WILL REDUCE OUR CHILDREN'S STANDARD OF LIVING

Even well-known and highly respected economics texts have fallen into this myth:

Perhaps the most serious consequence of a large public debt is that it displaces capital from the nation's stock of wealth. As a result, the pace of economic growth slows and future living standards will decline.[14] . . . the national debt will be a burden if it is sold to foreigners or contracted in a fully employed peacetime economy. In the latter case it will reduce the nation's capital stock.[15]

The claim here is that funds borrowed by the government contribute less to our future standard of living than the same funds invested by private firms.[16] This logic is correct if the government spends the borrowed funds on consumption. But if the government invests, the result is unclear. Both public investment and private investment increase our stock of capital (physical and human) and thereby enhance future productivity and income. Sometimes public investment is more beneficial for our children than private investment.[17]

MYTH 10. DEFICITS CROWD OUT PRIVATE INVESTMENT

Whether a deficit crowds out private investment depends on the state of the economy and the Fed's reaction.

If the government runs a deficit when the economy is booming, the Fed will push up interest rates to offset the effects of deficit spending and prevent inflation. If the Fed succeeds in blocking an increase in total spending, the higher interest rates will have "crowded out" private investment. But if the Fed is unsuccessful in preventing an increase in total spending, then private investment may rise or fall, since more spending stimulates businesses to invest, while higher interest rates depress investment.

If a deficit is incurred while the economy is in a recession, the Fed is unlikely to push up interest rates. In that case, deficit spending, by increasing total spending, will stimulate private investment.[18]

MYTH 11. INTEREST ON THE PUBLIC DEBT CROWDS OUT OTHER GOVERNMENT SPENDING

As the late *Washington Post* columnist Hobart Rowen put it:

Every dollar paid on interest on the accumulated debt is a dollar that can't be spent on health care, highways, or other federal programs.[19]

Unraveling this myth requires more discussion than the others, so bear with me.

At the most simplistic level, the myth is false. Our federal government, unlike a household, has an unlimited credit line as well as the constitutional power to tax. It therefore has the legal authority to increase spending whatever the size of the debt. Knowledgeable observers like Hobart Rowen know this, of course.

So what did Rowen mean? He meant that interest payments on the debt eat up such a large proportion of our taxes (17% in 1995)[20] that vital government programs are crowded out. Why crowded out? Because there's no politically feasible way to pay for them. Voters don't want a tax increase, and federal borrowing has become taboo.

So, how do we scale down the interest payments on the debt? The deficit hawks want us to cut the deficit by decreasing government spending and raising taxes. At first glance, this solution seems paradoxical: cut government spending even though vital projects require additional government spending? Raise taxes even though people want tax cuts?

The deficit hawks are thinking long-run. It took years of huge deficits to create the heavy interest payments. It will take years to shrink them. The deficit hawks see our national situation as analogous to that of a family who has overused its credit cards for years and now has to tighten its belt for years to restore a healthy debt–income ratio.

The deficit hawks want to cut the deficit by decreasing consumption, either by cutting entitlement spending or by raising taxes on consumers. Such fiscal actions by themselves would depress total spending and cause an economic slump. The Fed would react to such a threat by pushing down interest rates, thus boosting private investment and reducing our indebtedness to foreigners.[21] Thus, the benefits of current consumption would be sacrificed in order to secure the future benefits of increased income and decreased foreign debt.

How would these actions shrink the proportion of tax revenues required to pay interest on the public debt? By boosting future tax revenues and decreasing future interest payments. Higher investment implies increased future incomes and thus more taxes. Smaller deficits slow the growth of the public debt and the interest payments required to service that debt. Consequently, a smaller proportion of our future taxes would be swallowed up by interest payments on the debt, the outcome desired by the deficit hawks.

So far so good, but the deficit hawks fail to mention the pitfalls inherent in such a policy.

- Our children might benefit more if the dollars switched out of consumption were spent on both private and public investment, instead of on private investment alone. In other words, we might help future generations more by eliminating only a portion of the deficit and switching the remaining government borrowing from consumption into public investment.[22]

- The deficit hawks have been so successful in convincing the public that the deficit must be eliminated that budget cuts are affecting public investment projects as well as consumption.[23] In their rush to balance the budget, politicians have been cutting such investments as research and job training along with entitlements. Our children's income could suffer as a result.

- Deficit hysteria could make the economy recession-prone.[24] A stagnant economy not only damages us but also injures future generations by discouraging private investment.

MYTH 12. THE SOLUTION IS A BALANCED BUDGET AMENDMENT TO THE CONSTITUTION

In June 1992, the House of Representatives failed by nine votes to achieve the two-thirds majority necessary to pass a balanced budget amendment to the U.S. Constitution. Such an amendment would require that the budget deficit have an annual value of zero.

One possible reason for the defeat of the amendment was that 471 economists, including seven Nobel Prize winners, signed a statement condemning it.[25] The nonpartisan Congressional Budget Office also opposed it.[26]

But the balanced budget amendment is far from dead. In late January 1995, it again came up for a vote. This time the House approved it by a vote of 300 to 132. On March 2, 1995, the Senate failed by one vote to adopt the amendment. Fourteen Democrats joined with 52 Republicans in the effort to pass it. At the last minute Senate Majority Leader Robert Dole of Kansas switched his vote to "no" in a parliamentary maneuver that would have enabled him to bring the amendment up again. Republicans consider the bill a top priority.

A balanced-budget amendment to the U.S. Constitution is, in my judgment, an irresponsible and dangerous idea. Here are some reasons:

1. Whenever the economy slips into a recession, an automatic deficit is created. Such a deficit pumps needed purchasing power into a slumping economy, diminishing the effects of the recession on income and employment.[27] A balanced budget amendment would require a cut in government spending or an increase in taxes to offset the automatic def-

icit.[28] The result would be a fiscal contraction, aggravating the loss of jobs and income. As the CBO put it, "such an amendment could hobble the ability of the federal government to stabilize the economy."[29] The statement of 471 economists also emphasized this danger:

When the private economy is in recession, a constitutional requirement that would force cuts in public spending or tax increases could worsen the economic downturn, causing greater loss of jobs, production, and income.[30]

2. The federal government would be unable to borrow for investment programs that could be of crucial importance for our children. Even if an investment program were to generate its benefits many decades into the future, Congress could pay for that program only out of current taxes. Thus, a balanced budget amendment would prevent the federal government from borrowing for such investments as highways, bridges, harbors, airports, schools, hospitals, prisons, military installations, worker training, public health, toxic waste cleanup, basic research, and technological innovation. (Note that state and local governments are subject to no such restriction.)

A frequent response to this concern is that these investment projects will devolve onto state and local governments. It is a pipe dream to imagine that state and local governments could fill the void created by declining federal investment projects. Because the benefits of these projects spill over onto other jurisdictions, state and local governments typically underinvest.

3. Congress would be driven to devise budget gimmicks to get around such an inflexible rule. What would prevent our lawmakers from "balancing the budget" by defining certain spending as "off-budget" or shifting payment dates or altering the timing of tax collections or postponing necessary spending? All these techniques have been used to fulfill the requirements of previous deficit-limiting laws, such as the Gramm–Rudman–Hollings Balanced Budget Act of 1985. An especially dangerous gimmick would be to exchange treasured national assets for revenue and count this revenue toward balancing the budget. Perhaps we could sell the Grand Canyon? Don't laugh. Sales of national assets have provided revenue for deficit reduction.[31]

I fear that a balanced budget amendment would work like Prohibition. It would be flagrantly violated, making a mockery of our Constitution. The CBO agrees. "The most important problem with a balanced budget rule is that it inevitably invites avoidance and evasion, as do all fixed annual deficit targets." The statement of 471 economists also stresses this danger. "The amendment would give rise to inappropriate uses of government mandates, regulations, tax breaks, and new forms of 'off-budget' spending designed to evade the amendment's rigid Constitutional restrictions on taxing and spending."

4. Since it is the function of the judiciary to interpret the Constitution, the courts would be forced to decide whether Congress was obeying a balanced budget amendment. The amendment would thus involve the courts in the determination of economic policy. Instead of elected officials, unelected judges with lifetime tenure would be making economic decisions. Moreover, "the slow, complex, and deliberate nature of the judicial process would severely undermine the need for economic policy to be flexible and rapid in response to changing conditions."[32]

Even economists who deplore the huge deficits of recent years believe that a balanced budget amendment to the U.S. Constitution would injure our economic well-being. That such an amendment would somehow solve our problems is perhaps the most dangerous myth of all.

NOTES

1. *Raleigh News and Observer*, February 2, 1993.

2. See Chapter 2, Section 2.

3. For a historical example see *Presidential Economics* by Herbert Stein, pp. 113–122.

4. See Chapter 2, Sections 4, 7, and 8 for discussions of monetary policy.

5. For an explanation of this relationship, see Chapter 3, Section 2.

6. Foreign purchases of U.S. assets jumped from around $87 billion in 1980 to $122.3 billion in 1982, while declining from almost $115 billion in 1989 to $62.2 billion in 1991. See the *Economic Report of the President*, January 1993, p. 463.

7. "What Do Budget Deficits Do?" by Lawrence Ball and Gregory Mankiw in *Budget Deficits and Debt: Issues and Options*, a symposium sponsored by the Federal Reserve Bank of Kansas City, 1995, p. 112.

8. "Solutions for Developed Economies" by Alberto Giovanni in *Budget Deficits and Debt: Issues and Options*, a symposium sponsored by the Federal Reserve Bank of Kansas City, 1995, p. 251.

9. *The Debt and the Deficit* by Robert Heilbroner and Peter Bernstein, p. 121.

10. "What Do Budget Deficits Do?" by Lawrence Ball and Gregory Mankiw in *Budget Deficits and Debt: Issues and Options*, a symposium sponsored by the Federal Reserve Bank of Kansas City, 1995, pp. 112–113.

11. *The Age of Diminished Expectations* by Paul Krugman, p. 186.

12. See Chapter 3.

13. See Chapter 3, Section 1. If the economy is in a recession, increasing the deficit even for consumption will boost income and thus investment. Thus, future GDP could be increased. In this case the future tax burden could rise or fall. See Chapter 2, Section 4 and Chapter 3, Section 4.

14. *Economics*, 14th ed., by Paul A. Samuelson and William D. Nordhaus, p. 633.

15. *Economics*, 7th ed., by William J. Baumol and Alan S. Blinder, p. 764.

16. See Chapter 2, Sections 2, 3.

17. In personal communications both Paul Samuelson and William Baumol agreed that if the government borrows for investment rather than consumption, the quotes may not be correct. See Chapter 3, Section 3.

18. See Chapter 2, Section 6.

19. *Washington Post*, February 3, 1993.

20. In 1995, interest payments on the public debt were $232 billion, and total federal tax revenues were $1.36 trillion. See *The Economic and Budget Outlook: Fiscal Years 1997–2006*, Congress of the United States, Congressional Budget Office, May 1996, pp. 10, 37.

21. See Chapter 3, Section 2.

22. See Chapter 3, Section 6.

23. See Chapter 3, Section 3.

24. See Chapter 2, Section 9.

25. Statement issued by the Economic Policy Institute of Washington, D.C., on June 24, 1992.

26. *Reducing the Deficit: Spending and Revenue Options*, Congress of the United States, Congressional Budget Office, February 1993, pp. 7–8.

27. For a discussion of automatic and structural deficits, see Chapter 2, Section 6.

28. The amendment can be suspended by a supermajority, that is, by a vote of three-fifths of *all* members of both houses, which includes absentees and nonvoters. Such a provision would allow a minority of legislators to paralyze any fiscal action departing from a balanced budget.

29. *Reducing the Deficit: Spending and Revenue Options*, Congress of the United States, Congressional Budget Office, February 1993, p. 8.

30. Statement issued by the Economic Policy Institute of Washington, D.C., on June 24, 1992.

31. See, for example, *Economics*, 7th ed., by William Baumol and Alan Blinder, p. 316, or *Day of Reckoning* by Benjamin Friedman, p. 279.

32. Statement of 471 economists issued by the Economic Policy Institute of Washington, D.C., on June 24, 1992.

10

Questions and Answers

When your friends find out you've read this book, they may ask you questions. In this final chapter I'd like to prepare you for such encounters. Here's the scene I have in mind. You've finished the book. You enjoyed it. You're convinced I'm right. You mention the book to a group of your friends, and their initial reaction is that you've been reeled in by a slick charlatan. They pelt you with questions, some of them hostile. You're on the griddle. You feel you have to defend the ideas in the book. Fortunately, you've read this chapter, so you're primed for the interrogation.

It might go something like this:

Q: What does this guy have to say?

A: The main point is that deficits are not always bad. Sometimes they're good. It depends how the government is spending the money. Deficit hysteria has done us a lot of harm.

Q: What *is* the deficit anyway?

A: It's when the federal government spends more than it collects in taxes and has to borrow the difference from the public by selling securities, such as Treasury bills or bonds. The deficit is the amount the government borrows.

Q: What's the difference between the deficit and the debt?

A: The debt—the public debt—is the total stock of government securities held by the public, including foreigners. The deficit is the increase in this stock over the course of a year.

Q: I don't see how deficits can ever be good.

A: Benavie makes three points:

- Whenever the country goes into a recession, a deficit automatically results because taxes drop and public assistance increases. This automatic deficit cushions the slump by giving people more spending money.
- In a severe recession, the only way to energize the economy may be to purposely increase the deficit.
- Borrowing for public investment may crowd out private investment, but in some cases public investment is a better use of the funds.

Q: Do other economists agree that increasing the deficit can get us out of a recession?

A: In a survey of several hundred economists, 91% agreed that deficits stimulate the economy.

Q: How has deficit hysteria harmed us?

A: In our drive to cut the deficit we have depressed spending. That has caused businesses to cut production and lay off workers. We have also sacrificed public investment projects that could be crucial to the well-being of our kids.

Q: So, I guess he's against the balanced budget amendment?

A: He thinks it would be a disaster. In fact, he believes that striving to balance the federal budget is crazy. The struggle to eliminate the deficit would make the economy prone to recessions. Forcing the government to balance its budget would prevent it from borrowing for any reason, no matter how worthwhile. State and local governments borrow for highways and colleges and water systems. Corporations borrow for factories and equipment. You and I borrow to buy a home or send our kids to college. So why shouldn't the federal government borrow? Other governments don't restrict themselves in this way.

And one final point: a balanced budget amendment would involve the courts in judging the constitutionality of budget proposals. What a mess that would be.

Q: Does he at least agree the debt had gotten out of hand?

A: The public debt is backed by the nation's income. In fact, the burden of the debt is defined as the ratio of the debt to national income. That ratio is now about 50%. The debt burden has been higher in the past, much higher. In 1953, it was 60%. In 1946, the debt exceeded the nation's income. In spite of warnings that these debt levels would impoverish future generations, it obviously didn't happen.

Q: Could we run deficits forever?

A: Even chronic deficits do not necessarily mean the debt will become more burdensome. For example, suppose the 1995 deficit were to increase by 5% a year forever. According to broadly accepted predictions by economists, the ratio of debt to national income would actually decline and stabilize at 46%. The point here is that our national income is also expected to continue growing.

Q: What about our kids? Don't deficits hurt them?

A: That depends on how the government uses the borrowed money. When the government borrows, it often deprives businesses of those funds. So businesses will invest less in factories and equipment, and that reduces our future productivity and hurts our children. But if the government invests the borrowed money in research or airports or rebuilding our inner cities, then our children's standard of living could be increased. In other words, the public investment may do more for our kids than the private investment. On the other hand, if the borrowing is only for the benefit of the current generation—for example, if it is spent on Social Security or Medicare or farm price supports—then the deficits could hurt our children.

Q: So, all deficits aren't the same?

A: Right, that's a major theme of the book. A key distinction is whether the borrowing creates an asset that increases our future standard of living or whether it creates only current benefits. Borrowing by corporations or state and local governments or households is not referred to as deficit spending, probably because it is clear that the other side of the debt is a long-lived asset, such as a factory or a highway or a home. With our federal government, on the other hand, any borrowing is labeled a deficit whether the spending is used to build an airport or to pay salaries. Benavie sees this unfortunate use of language as one of the causes of deficit panic.

Q: Why should the government borrow money for airports or rebuilding inner cities? Why not pay for them out of taxes?

A: We could, but it's unlikely we would agree to such an arrangement. Think about the vast sums involved. Would you be willing to fork over huge hunks of your income in taxes to pay the cost of such long-lasting projects? It seems reasonable that since the benefits of these investments are distributed over future generations, the costs should likewise be distributed. That means borrowing. Do people purchase a house out of their current income? No, they borrow. Do corporations finance the construction of a factory out of their current revenues? No, they borrow.

Q: But our kids will have to pay interest on the government's debt. Won't that be a burden on them?

A: If the government spends the borrowed money in ways that increase the productivity of our workers, then the additional income of the nation could more than compensate for the costs of the debt.

Q: Is Benavie in favor of running deficits forever?

A: Yes, but only if the borrowed money is used wisely, is sufficiently productive, and is spent only for the benefit of future generations. Studies have shown that carefully chosen public investment projects can raise our future standard of living by more than private investment. Also many economists stress the critical need for more public investment in new technology, worker training, children's health, and infrastructure.

Q: What about the trillions of dollars of debt we are leaving to our children? Won't they have to pay it off?

A: No politician is calling for the elimination of the entire public debt. They have been urging a balanced budget, that is, the elimination of increases in the debt. Keep in mind that the debt consists of Treasury securities, which are assets to their owners. Our children inherit the debt, but they also inherit most of those assets, those not held by foreigners. Like corporations, governments never have to pay off the debt, and they don't. They simply "roll it over," that is, replace maturing debt with new debt. To retire government securities would entail the disappearance of the safest and highest-quality asset available to individuals, businesses, money market funds, pension funds, and state and local governments. Also, our central bank, the Fed, conducts monetary policy by buying and selling Treasury securities.

Q: Don't deficits cause high interest rates?

A: Not necessarily. In a recession the Fed will drive interest rates down to stimulate the economy whether the deficit is rising or falling. Only at full employment do increases in the deficit cause interest rates to go up. Historically, interest rates have not varied with the deficit.

Q: How about our debt to foreign countries? Isn't that related to the deficit?

A: Again, not necessarily. A major reason foreigners become our creditors is the level of our interest rates. When our interest rates rise, foreigners buy more of our assets. This happens whatever the deficit is doing.

Q: This guy sounds like he's coming from left field. I've heard lots of economists say we should eliminate the deficit.

A: Benavie mentions several reasons economists would talk like that:

- Some have been swept up in deficit hysteria. After all, even economists are human.
- Some are reluctant to publicly challenge the conventional wisdom that deficits are evil, because they're afraid to appear radical or irresponsible.
- Some use the deficit panic as a way of pushing their own political views.
- Some are called economists but actually have had little training in economics and may not understand the deficit. After all, anyone can hang up a shingle and call him or herself an economist. It's not like medicine or law.
- Economics has many different specialties. Some of these areas have little to do with the deficit. Therefore, it's possible to be an economist and not be familiar with the economics of the deficit.
- Many economists were disturbed by the huge Reagan–Bush deficits. They feel that the current generation benefited from that orgy of borrowing, while the tab was left for their children. They want to make sure that doesn't happen again.
- Finally, economists may agree on economics and yet have different views about economic policy, which involves values as well. For example, should we borrow to invest in our national parks or in space exploration, or should we leave these funds to businesses to invest in equipment and housing? Economists don't necessarily see eye-to-eye on questions like these. Those who favor private investment will be more critical of deficit spending.

Q: So, what does he think we should do?

A: He thinks we should make a big change in how we keep the federal books. We should have two budgets, a current budget and a capital budget. The current budget would be for consumption—Social Security, Medicare, government salaries, things that generate benefits right now. This budget would normally be balanced; that is, the spending would be paid for out of taxes. The capital budget would be for public investment projects—interstate highways, research, worker training, things that generate benefits in the future. The capital budget would be financed by borrowing.

Q: How would that help?

A: That way we would know what we were borrowing for. Right now there's no way to know whether we're borrowing for defense, for interest on the debt, or for farm price supports.

Q: What about a surplus? What does he think we should do if we end up with a surplus?

A: Well, we could eliminate the surplus by cutting taxes or increasing spending. That would have the same effect as increasing the deficit. The result would depend on what taxes we cut or how we spent the money. The right government investments could benefit our children more than if we protected the surplus (paid down the debt). On the other hand, protecting the surplus stimulates the private sector to invest, which would also boost our children's standard of living.

Q: Is this guy some kind of kook?

A: He doesn't seem to be. He quotes a lot of mainstream sources to back up his arguments—the Congressional Budget Office, Federal Reserve Banks, advisers to presidents, and some very well known economists. Read the book yourself. See what you think.

Selected Bibliography

Baily, Martin Neil, Burtless, Gary, and Litan, Robert E. *Growth with Equity*. Washington, D.C.: Brookings Institution, 1993.

Baumol, William J., and Blinder, Alan S. *Economics*, 7th ed. Fort Worth: Dryden Press, Harcourt, Brace, 1997.

Blinder, Alan S. *Hard Heads, Soft Hearts*. Reading, Mass.: Addison-Wesley, 1987.

Buchanan, James M., and Wagner, Richard E. *Democracy in Deficit: The Political Legacy of Lord Keynes*. New York: Academic Press, 1977.

Cannon, Lou. *President Reagan—The Role of a Lifetime*. New York: Simon & Schuster, 1991.

Cavanaugh, Francis X. *The Truth about the National Debt*. Cambridge, Mass.: Harvard Business School Press, 1996.

Cohen, Linda R., and Noll, Roger G. *The Technology Pork Barrel*. Washington, D.C.: Brookings Institution, 1991.

Dionne, E. J., Jr. *They Only Look Dead*. New York: Simon & Schuster, 1996.

Drew, Elizabeth. *On the Edge—The Clinton Presidency*. New York: Simon & Schuster, 1994.

———. *Showdown*. New York: Simon & Schuster, 1996.

Dunlop, John B. *The Rise of Russia and the Fall of the Soviet Empire*. Princeton, N.J.: Princeton University Press, 1993.

Edsall, Thomas B., and Edsall, Mary D. *Chain Reaction*. New York: W. W. Norton, 1991.

Eisner, Robert. *How Real Is the Federal Deficit?* New York: Free Press, 1986.

———. *The Misunderstood Economy*. Cambridge, Mass.: Harvard Business School Press, 1994.

Friedman, Benjamin M. *Day of Reckoning*. New York: Vintage Books, 1989.

Galbraith, John Kenneth. *The Good Society*. Boston: Houghton Mifflin, 1996.

Golay, Michael, and Rollyson, Carl. *Where America Stands—1996*. New York: John Wiley & Sons, 1996.

Heilbroner, Robert, and Bernstein, Peter. *The Debt and the Deficit*. New York: W. W. Norton, 1989.

Heilbroner, Robert, and Thurow, Lester. *Economics Explained*. New York: Simon & Schuster, 1994.

Keech, William R. *Economic Politics*. New York: Cambridge University Press, 1995.

Keynes, John Maynard. *The General Theory of Employment, Interest and Money*. New York: Harcourt Brace Jovanovich, 1936.

Kotlikoff, Lawrence. *Generational Accounting*. New York: Free Press, 1992.

Krugman, Paul. *The Age of Diminished Expectations*. Cambridge, Mass.: MIT Press, 1992.

———. *Peddling Prosperity*. New York: W. W. Norton, 1994.

Makin, John H, and Ornstein, Norman J. *Debt and Taxes*. New York: Times Books, 1994.

Morgan, Iwan W. *Deficit Government*. Chicago: Ivan R. Dee, 1995.

Peterson, Wallace C. *Silent Depression*. New York: W. W. Norton, 1994.

Peterson, Peter G. *Facing Up*. New York: Simon & Schuster, 1993.

———. *Will America Grow Up Before It Grows Old?* New York: Random House, 1996.

Rivlin, Alice M. *Reviving the American Dream*. Washington, D.C.: Brookings Institution, 1992.

Rock, James M., ed. *Debt and the Twin Deficits Debate*. Mountain View, Calif.: Bristlecone Books, Mayfield, 1991.

Samuelson, Paul A., and Nordhaus, William D. *Economics*, 14th ed. New York: McGraw-Hill, 1992.

Samuelson, Robert J. *The Good Life and Its Discontents*. New York: Times Books, 1995.

Savage, James D. *Balanced Budgets and American Politics*. Ithaca, N.Y.: Cornell University Press, 1988.

Schultze, Charles L. *Memos to the President*. Washington, D.C.: Brookings Institution, 1992.

Skidelsky, Robert. *John Maynard Keynes*. New York: Penguin Press, 1994.

Stein, Herbert. *Presidential Economics*. Washington, D.C.: American Enterprise Institute, 1994.

Sundquist, James L. *Politics and Policy: The Eisenhower, Kennedy, and Johnson Years*. Washington, D.C.: Brookings Institution, 1968.

White, Joseph, and Wildavsky, Aaron. *The Deficit and the Public Interest*. Berkeley, Calif.: University of California Press, 1989.

Woodward, Bob. *The Agenda*. New York: Simon & Schuster, 1994.

Index

About the Author

ARTHUR BENAVIE is Professor of Economics at the University of North Carolina at Chapel Hill. His specialty is macroeconomics, which includes the topic of the deficit. He has published numerous journal articles and two books for economists.